Gaining Funding for Research
A Guide for Academics and Institutions

Gaining Funding for Research

A Guide for Academics and Institutions

Dianne C. Berry

 Open University Press

Open University Press
McGraw-Hill Education
McGraw-Hill House
Shoppenhangers Road
Maidenhead
Berkshire
England
SL6 2QL

email: enquiries@openup.co.uk
world wide web: www.openup.co.uk

and Two Penn Plaza, New York, NY 10121-2289, USA

First published 2010

A catalogue record of this book is available from the British Library

ISBN-13: 978-0-335-23658-9 (pb) 978-0-335-23659-6 (hb)
ISBN-10: 0335236588 (pb) 0335236596 (hb)

Library of Congress Cataloging-in-Publication Data
CIP data applied for

Typeset by RefineCatch Limited, Bungay, Suffolk
Printed in the UK by Bell & Bain Ltd, Glasgow

Mixed Sources
Product group from well-managed
forests and other controlled sources
www.fsc.org Cert no. TT-COC-002769
© 1996 Forest Stewardship Council

The McGraw·Hill Companies

Contents

Preface

So why did I agree to write this book? It was not as if I was looking for something to fill my spare hours, as I had no spare hours. The reason was that I believed there was a genuine need for such a book. Researchers today are under increasing pressure to secure external grant income to fund their research. But at the same time they are facing increasing competition from others in the same position. The need to submit well prepared, truly competitive applications has never been greater. This book will help you to do just that. But hopefully it will do more than this, in that it places the 'grant getting business' within a much wider context, both within your institution and externally. It also looks at grant winning as part of the overall process of career development and establishing yourself as a leading researcher.

So why did I feel qualified to write the book? The main reason is that I have experienced the grant getting process from all sides. As Pro-Vice-Chancellor for Research, I have been responsible for working with colleagues across the University to ensure that my university improves the standing of its research and increases the level of external income that it secures to support this. This involves thinking about what does and does not motivate researchers, what facilitates them and what hinders them, and what support the University needs to provide to help them. From a research funding organization perspective, I have acted as a referee and sat on the funding committees and panels for three of the UK Research Councils, as well as other funders. And finally, of course, I have experienced the grant getting process, and building a research career, from the perspective of an individual researcher in terms of preparing my own applications, gaining grants and, unfortunately, sometimes having to cope with rejection.

I decided to start this book by setting some context to provide an understanding of why it is so important to gain external research funding, both from an institutional perspective and from the perspective of an individual researcher. Chapter 1 therefore outlines how universities are currently funded and looks particularly at the Dual Support system in the UK. It also discusses pressures on institutions to secure external funding, including the increasing costs of supporting research. I also wanted to think about what constitutes research, and look at different types of research and the different settings in which it can take place, and this is covered in Chapter 2.

A key part of gaining funding is to find an appropriate funding source. Chapters 3 and 4 look at the main sources of research funding available for

UK based researchers. Chapter 3 focuses on the UK Research Councils as these are the major funders in the UK, supporting almost 40 per cent of university based research across the sector. Chapter 4 looks at a wide range of other funders, including charities, trusts, professional associations, the European Union, and business and industry. The chapters also outline the different modes of funding available to researchers, such as research grants and programmes, fellowships, networks, and larger centres.

One thing you need to know when preparing any grant application is how your proposal will be assessed. Chapter 5 looks at the peer review process, how this works, and the criteria that are typically used. It considers the validity of the process and how key funding organizations are responding to increasing pressure on the peer review system. It also looks at how grants committees and panels typically operate.

Chapter 6 is aimed at helping new researchers who are inexperienced in the grant winning business. It provides a guide for how to get started in terms of applying for research funding, what sources of help there are, and how to start to build up a track record. It outlines the main funding schemes that are specifically aimed at supporting new researchers and how to increase chances of success in these. Following on from this, Chapter 7 looks further at how to improve chances of success in gaining funding, irrespective of your level of experience. It looks in detail at how to structure a proposal and present your ideas in the most appropriate and convincing way. The chapter includes some examples of 'good practice' in terms of writing abstracts and summaries, aims and objectives, dissemination and time management plans, and justifying resources. Finally, it provides advice about how best to take account of, and respond to, reviewers' comments, again with examples of good practice. It is necessary to ensure that all research is conducted in line with relevant ethical standards and principles and, in many areas, it is necessary to gain approval from one or more Research Ethics Committees for projects to go ahead. The process of doing this is covered in Chapter 8.

Preparing a good application involves getting the budget right. Chapter 9 looks at what is involved in costing and pricing research and formulating and justifying budgets. It explains the full economic costing methodology, and why institutions need to have a pricing policy, and shows examples of how to translate a list of resources needed to carry out a project into a costed application form. Finally, Chapter 10 considers how to move on from initial success at winning your first grant to establishing a research group and building up a successful track record of gaining funding. It looks at what is involved in research management and leadership, and how to play a role in shaping the funding agenda. It also considers diversifying funding sources, working with business and industry and commercializing research findings.

By the end of the book, I would hope that you have a much better feel for why it is important to gain funding, how you might start out, how to improve your chances of success irrespective of your level of experience, and how you can move on to establish a reputation and become a research leader in your field. Clearly, a book of this length cannot cover all possible information and sources of advice. I have therefore included Appendix 1, which outlines the main sources of further information that you can draw on to supplement what is included here. Appendix 1 features a detailed list of websites, many of which contain useful guides and other documents, as well as recommended further reading.

Many people have contributed to my inspiration for, and writing of, this book. This includes many colleagues at Reading University; from those who have attended new lecturers' courses, through discipline level directors of research, to other senior managers. It also includes staff in our Research and Enterprise Services Directorate, particularly the Research Support team. My thinking has also benefited from discussions with colleagues at other universities, with whom I have worked on grants committees, and other forms of assessment panel, as well as the many people with whom I have worked who are based within the research funding organizations themselves.

I am particularly grateful to Professor John Harris and two anonymous reviewers, who provided very helpful comments on an earlier draft of this book. Their suggestions were invaluable in producing what I hope will be a very useful text. I am also grateful to Professor Michael Ball and Dr Christopher Stokes for allowing me to use excerpts from their successful grants proposals as examples of good practice, and to a range of other researchers whose successful proposals provided the basis for my constructing many of the hypothetical, but nevertheless realistic, examples that are also included in the book.

I very much hope this book brings you success.

Abbreviations

AHRC	Arts and Humanities Research Council
AMRC	Association of Medical Research Charities
ARC	Australian Research Council
BBSRC	Biotechnology and Biological Sciences Research Council
BERA	British Educational Research Association
BHF	British Heart Foundation
BPS	British Psychological Society
BSA	British Sociological Association
CASE	Collaborative Awards in Science and Engineering
CCLRC	Council for the Central Laboratory of the Research Councils
CORDIS	Community Research and Development Information Service
COS	Community of Science
DEFRA	Department for Environment, Food and Rural Affairs
DENI	Department of Education Northern Ireland
DERA	Defence Evaluation and Research Agency
DIUS	Department for Innovation, Universities and Skills
DSTL	Defence Science and Technology Laboratory
EAA	Electronic Applications and Assessment
EAPC	Euro-Atlantic Partnership Council
EPSRC	Engineering and Physical Sciences Research Council
ERC	European Research Council
ESRC	Economic and Social Research Council
FDA	Federal Drugs Administration (US)
fEC	full economic costing
HEFCE	Higher Education Funding Council for England
HEFCW	Higher Education Funding Council for Wales
HEI	higher education institution
HEIF	Higher Education Innovation Fund
HR	Human Resources
HTD	Health Technology Devices
IP	intellectual property
IPA	Industrial Partnership Award
IRAS	Integrated Research Application System
ISIS	International Science Interchange Scheme
JCPSG	Joint Costing and Pricing Steering Group
JIF	Joint Infrastructure Fund

KTN	Knowledge Transfer Network
KTP	Knowledge Transfer Partnership
LOLA	Longer Larger Awards scheme
MICA	MRC Industry Collaborative Award
MOD	Ministry of Defence
MRC	Medical Research Council
NEAT	New and Emerging Applications of Technology
NERC	Natural Environment Research Council
NHS	National Health Service
NIHR	National Institute of Health Research
NRES	National Research Ethics Service
PI	principal investigator
PPSRC	Particle and Physics and Astronomy Research Council
QR	Quality related funding
RAE	Research assessment exercise
R&D	Research and development
RCIF	Research Capital Investment Fund
RCUK	Research Councils UK
REC	research ethics committee
REF	Research Excellence Framework
RfPB	Research for Patient Benefit
RISC	Research for Innovation, Speculation and Creativity
SERC	Science and Engineering Research Council
SFC	Scottish Funding Council
SME	small and medium size enterprises
SRIF	Science Research Infrastructure scheme
STFC	Science and Technology Facilities Council
TRAC	Transparent Approach to Costing
TSB	Technology Strategy Board
UKRO	UK Research Office

1

Setting the scene

University funding for research • Dual Support System • The need for reform • TRAC and the move to full economic costing • Capital funding for research • The importance of gaining external funding for research

Engaging in research costs money. This may seem strikingly obvious but it is only in relatively recent years that academia has truly recognized this and is taking account of it when formulating budgetary and management processes. There is now increasing pressure on both institutions, and individuals within them, to raise funding to support research, either directly through external grants and contracts and/or indirectly via performing well in exercises such as the UK's Research Assessment Exercise (RAE) and, in future, the Research Excellence Framework. The ability to attract large amounts of external research income is becoming a key criterion when appointing new academic staff, and universities compete highly to recruit those with the strongest track records and who come with the largest dowries. Virtually gone are the days when a long list of high quality publications was sufficient to secure that all important job. Appointments and promotions committees are increasingly turning their attention to the grant funding section of CVs.

So what has brought about this change? A primary reason is the steady reduction in the relative amount of core 'unrestricted' funding that is allocated to universities from Government. This has put increasing pressure on institutions to find alternative sources of income to cover their costs and support their academic mission. Hand in hand with this in the UK has been the rise in the dominance of the Research Assessment Exercise and the increasingly selective allocation of research funding, with larger amounts of money being channelled into fewer institutions. In order to retain a reputation for being 'research intensive', universities have to ensure that their staff not only produce first class research outputs but that they also gain substantial research income and recruit good numbers of postgraduate research students. This in turn puts pressure on major research funders, who are seeing significant increases in numbers of applications in recent years and a concomitant fall in success rates. In mid-2009 several of the UK Research Councils were reporting that success rates had dropped below 20 per cent, and in some rounds were as low as 10 per cent. Many of the major research funders, including some of the Research Councils, have also moved towards allocating some funding streams in a more concentrated manner, supporting those who have strong track records and existing portfolios of activity. Most also publish annual league tables showing institutional performance in terms of numbers (and amounts) of new awards and success rates (see Chapter 3), again putting pressure on poorer performing universities to 'up their game'. More generally, we are increasingly steeped in a league table culture, where performance on these measures is available for all to see, and to take into account when selecting where to study, where to work and, in the case of research sponsors, whom to fund. As noted in a report by the Higher Education Funding Council for England (HEFCE 2008), league tables are an inevitable part of the higher education landscape and newspaper calendar.

It also has to be recognized that in many areas, particularly in the sciences, research is becoming increasingly expensive to conduct. Scientific and technological advances mean that much of today's research requires the use of equipment and other major facilities that can cost from tens of thousands to many millions of pounds. On top of this there will often be significant additional costs for consumables, such as expensive chemicals and compounds, that are necessary to carry out the day to day laboratory work. Even within the arts and humanities disciplines, where researchers have traditionally stated that they do not need funding in order to carry out their research, the increasing costs of housing and maintaining libraries and specialist research collections, and of providing access to the wealth of research information and outputs available electronically, add to the pressure on institutions to secure more external funding. They can no longer afford to fund the range of research they engage in from internal sources.

As a result of, but also contributing to, this change in academic culture have been the increasingly rigorous internal research management processes that have been put in place within institutions. There is now much more awareness and monitoring of the research performance of individual staff and groups. The decision about whether or not, or the extent to which, one engages in research and applies for research funding is no longer a private matter for individual academics. Application, award and success rates are routinely monitored by institutions. In some cases, individual staff members are given specific targets to reach as part of the ongoing appraisal of their performance. For most, academic life is now very different from what it would have been in the 1990s, let alone 50 years earlier. As noted in a report for HEFCE by Evidence (2005), the model of the lone academic has increasingly been replaced by one of managed environments. Activities that might once have been left to individual academic researchers are now more closely integrated with strategic corporate objectives. The classification of staff or departments as 'research active' or 'research inactive' has become central to an understanding of academic identity and the positioning and valuing of academic work and department status (Lucas 2006).

Effective research management involves both academic and administrative support. According to the Association of Commonwealth Universities, research management embraces anything that universities can do to maximize the impact of their research activity. It includes assistance in formulating research ideas into fundable proposals, identifying new sources of funds, presenting research applications convincingly, and providing advice on costing projects and negotiating contracts with external sponsors. It also incorporates project management and financial control systems, and involves help in exploiting research results – through commercialization, knowledge exchange and dissemination to wider society (Association of Commonwealth Universities 2008).

It can be seen that developing and sustaining a broad research portfolio is far from straightforward these days. The landscape in which funding for research is applied for and won has become increasingly competitive and global in nature. Universities that are successful at winning research funding are now required to fulfil a range of obligations, in that research grants and contracts are increasingly monitored and audited by funders and are often tied to specific milestones and deliverables. According to Green and Langley (2009), increased competitiveness, complexity and scrutiny within the research arena have created a need to manage the research portfolio more closely.

University funding for research

Before describing different sources of funding for research, it is worth noting that while a great many universities define themselves in terms of their research standing and being a research university, the majority of these actually get far more of their funding for teaching than for research. My own university, for example, receives 50 per cent more income from HEFCE to support its teaching than its research. Additional income from UK tuition fees and overseas student fees means that the balance is heavily distorted. Across all universities, HEFCE awarded £4782 million for learning and teaching in 2009/ 10, compared with £1572 million for research. A similar pattern is present across the other UK funding councils, with Scotland, for example, awarding over £700 million for teaching compared with less than £300 million for research. This imbalance has led to an interesting dilemma in many universities, with it often being commented that while teaching pays for most academics' jobs, it is research which makes their careers. As Clark (1994) no 'research is of prime importance in academics' value systems . . . and university reward and value systems are premised on achievement in research. Yet the formulae by which universities are block funded are usually premised on teaching activities. Academics must teach but they prefer to engage in research' (Clark 1994: 15). Clearly this is not the case for all academics, but there is nevertheless a lot of truth in the statement.

University research is typically funded from a range of different sources. With the exception of private universities, government is the key funder for the majority of institutions. In the UK there are two streams of government funding for research: one which is in the form of an unrestricted block grant and is awarded by the Funding Councils (HEFCE in England, SFC in Scotland, HEFCW in Wales and DENI in Northern Ireland), and one which generally is in the form of project and programme grants and is allocated by the Research Councils. The combination of the two streams is known as the Dual Support System. Across the sector, universities get around 55 to 60 per cent of their research income via the two streams in the Dual Support System. It is worth noting that a number of other countries (e.g. Canada, Australia, New Zealand) have similar dual funding systems, although the proportion of funding going into each stream, and the basis on which allocations are determined, vary from country to country. What these countries also have in common is the fact that the proportion of funding going into the 'unrestricted' leg of the funding has diminished considerably in recent years, a point which will be expanded on below. Many universities may also have some additional sources of 'unrestricted' funding for research, such as from Trust funds and endowments, bequests, and income from sale of university assets. Typically though, these amounts, in total, are far smaller than the unrestricted funding that comes from central government.

In addition to this unrestricted funding, most institutions will receive grant and contract income from a range of other public and private funders. This income is generally awarded to support research on specific projects, and is therefore more restricted in terms of its use. In the UK the main sponsors of research projects and programmes, in addition to the Research Councils, are charities, government departments, industry and commerce, the European Union, and some professional bodies. Across the sector, around 20 per cent of university research income comes from UK charities, around 15 per cent from government departments, around 8 per cent from UK industry, and around 10 per cent from the EU. Universities are increasingly looking to support their research from a diverse range of funding sources.

As a result of diminishing amounts of unrestricted funding and increasing competition for restricted funding for research, many universities have also been attempting to support some forms of research activity (such as research chairs, or support for new research centres or institutes) from private fundraising and sponsorship. US universities have a much longer, and more successful, history of doing this, but UK universities are increasingly setting up new development or fund-raising offices, with experienced personnel, in order to bring a professional approach to their fund-raising activities. Drawing on his US experience, David Ward, former president of the American Council on Education, told the 2009 Annual HEFCE Conference that universities can no longer afford to sustain a comprehensive portfolio of research simply on the basis of public funding (Ward 2009). In order to encourage universities in their fund-raising activities, HEFCE recently introduced a Government-led matched funding scheme to increase voluntary giving to higher education institutions. The scheme runs from 2008 to 2011, and provides matched funding for 'eligible gifts' to English universities.

Dual Support System

The logic behind the UK's Dual Support System is that it provides two distinct, but related, sources of income for university research. The Research Councils support basic, strategic and applied research across a wide range of disciplines. They fund specific projects and programmes on a competitive basis, as well as funding their own specific institutes in many cases. They are able to take a national strategic view, balancing directive and responsive support and ensuring excellence through peer review. They also provide funding for postgraduate research training, increasingly through some form of Doctoral Training Award (DTA) to institutions. The size of these awards is determined (either solely or partly) by the amount of grant income awarded to the institution by the Council. Thus, institutions who are more successful at winning competitive grant income from a particular Research Council will also receive more funding to support postgraduate research students.

In contrast, the Funding Councils' allocation of Quality Related (QR) funding is primarily informed by the results of the RAE. The first such exercise was carried out in 1986, and there have been five further rounds since then, with the most recent taking place in 2008. The nature of the exercise has changed over the years but, at a basic level, each has involved assessing the quality of research (with most emphasis on publications and other outputs) based on the judgement of academic peers. On the positive side, the RAE has been said to raise levels of research activity and standards within UK universities, and has also provided an impetus for universities to improve the organization and management of their research. Critics, however, have argued that the intrinsic value of research for academics has been replaced by pressure to maximize the RAE value of their research (e.g. Harvie 2000). The RAE has also been criticized for being overly bureaucratic and costly to operate. Partly as a result of these criticisms, the RAE is being replaced by a new Research Excellence Framework (REF), with the first full exercise being planned for 2013. The REF will involve greater use of bibliometric data and other research related metrics, and will also put more emphasis on assessing the broader economic, social and cultural impact of research in addition to its academic impact. A key metric will be the amount of external grant income awarded to the institution.

Performance in the RAE, and in future the REF, has and will determine QR funding allocations to institutions. In the current system, allocations are weighted according to performance in the RAE, a volume measure (determined by the number of research active staff submitted in each unit), and the cost bracket for the area of research in question. Up until 2009–10, allocations were driven by performance in the 2001 RAE, with units rated below 4 typically receiving no funding, and those rated as 5* receiving almost four times as much funding as those rated 4 (for the same volume of activity and in the same subject centre cost bracket). Although, in England, HEFCE's policy was not to fund research in units rated below 4, it identified a number of emerging subject areas (art and design, communication, culture and media studies; dance, drama and performing arts; nursing, social work, other studies and professions allied to medicine; and sports related studies) where the research base was not as strong as in more established areas. HEFCE established a Research Capability Fund that provided support to units rated 3a and 3b in these specific subject areas. In the 2008 RAE, the methodology was changed so that, rather than assessing units by giving them a 'score' on a scale ranging from 1 to 5*, quality was reflected as a profile showing the proportion of research activity at each level of excellence (ranging from unclassified to world leading – 4*). Funding was again selectively allocated, with unclassified and 1* activity receiving no funding, 3* receiving three times as much as 2*, and 4* receiving seven times as much as 2* (with this being increased to nine times in 2010/11). The overall quality profile for each institutional unit was a weighted combination of three separate profiles, one reflecting the assessment of research outputs, one reflecting assessment of the research environment and the third reflecting assessment of indicators of esteem. One component of the environment assessment was the amount of external grant income gained by the unit over the assessment period, again reflecting the importance of winning grant income for the institution.

Linking the allocation of QR funding to the RAE is said to be a way of ensuring that the limited government funding for research that is available is used to reward excellence, as determined by peer review. It provides a (necessary) level of selectivity in funding, but does not simply allocate income to a small number of 'top' institutions. Rather, the underlying principle is that funding is used to support excellence wherever this is found. Having said this, the majority of QR (unlike funding for teaching) is concentrated in relatively few institutions. In 2007/8, over 75 per cent of QR funding was allocated to just 23 institutions. At the other end of the scale, around 40 universities have five per cent or less of their income from QR funding (Lucas 2006). Interestingly (and not surprisingly), the allocation of Research Council funding is equally selective, with over 80 per cent of funding in 2007/8 being allocated to just 20 institutions. These proportions have not changed substantially in more recent years. Not surprisingly, there is considerable overlap between the institutions who perform best in the RAE and those who gain the most competitively awarded grant income. Tables 1.1 and 1.2 show the top 20 institutions in the UK, in terms of RAE performance and grant income won from the UK Research Councils and Wellcome Trust (the largest research charity in the UK). It can be seen that 16 universities appear in both lists, with the same five institutions ranking in the top six in both lists.

Table 1.1 The top 20 Higher Education Institutions (excluding specialist units) in terms of performance in the 2008 Research Assessment Exercise (percentage of activity rated at each of the five quality levels)

Rank	Institution	4*	3*	2*	1*	UC
1	University of Cambridge	32	39	24	4	1
2	London School of Economics	35	34	25	6	1
2	University of Oxford	32	39	24	5	1
4	Imperial College, London	26	47	23	4	0
5	University College, London	27	39	27	6	1
6	University of Manchester	23	42	29	6	0
7	University of Warwick	21	44	29	6	0
8	University of York	23	39	31	6	0
9	University of Essex	22	41	30	7	0
10	University of Edinburgh	22	40	28	8	2
11	Queen Mary, University of London	19	44	29	8	0
12	Durham University	20	41	31	8	1
12	University of St Andrews	19	40	34	6	0
12	University of Sheffield	19	42	32	7	0
12	University of Southampton	18	43	32	7	0
12	University of Leeds	18	43	33	6	0
12	University of Bristol	18	43	31	7	0
18	University of Bath	19	41	33	7	0
18	Lancaster University	19	42	31	8	0
20	Cardiff University	19	40	32	9	0
20	Kings College, London	19	41	32	8	1

Table 1.2 The top 20 HEIs in terms of success in winning research grants from the UK Research Councils and Wellcome Trust from 2005–6 to 2007–8

Rank	Institution	Total Research Council awards £m	Total Wellcome Trust awards £m	Total grant awards from both sources £m
1	University of Cambridge	358.1	119.5	477.6
2	University of Oxford	312.3	159.0	471.3
3	Imperial College, London	316.5	66.0	382.5
4	University College, London	285.7	87.3	373.0
5	University of Manchester	282.6	35.5	318.1
6	University of Edinburgh	200.0	58.9	258.9
7	University of Bristol	156.8	23.2	180.0
8	University of Nottingham	154.5	7.7	162.2

(Continued Overleaf)

Table 1.2 Continued

Rank	Institution	Total Research Council awards £m	Total Wellcome Trust awards £m	Total grant awards from both sources £m
9	University of Leeds	149.7	10.5	160.2
10	University of Glasgow	138.5	18.6	157.1
11	University of Southampton	143.5	5.3	148.8
12	University of Sheffield	139.8	8.6	148.4
13	University of Birmingham	128.9	11.4	140.3
14	University of Warwick	135.2	4.3	139.5
15	Kings College, London	94.6	29.9	124.5
16	University of Newcastle	95.4	12.0	107.4
17	University of Liverpool	88.2	11.5	99.7
18	Cardiff University	81.2	10.1	91.3
19	University of Durham	87.9	1.9	89.8
20	University of Bath	69.5	5.6	75.1

In addition to the RAE related component of QR, there are a number of other smaller components. In England, there is a strand to fund postgraduate research (PGR) students, a strand determined by the amount of research income from industry and commerce, and a strand to support work commissioned by UK research charities. This latter strand relates to income that has been awarded through peer review and in open competition. In 2009/10 the amounts of HEFCE QR going into these three strands were £203 million, £63 million, and £194 million for the PGR, business and charity components respectively. This charity component is strongly supported by Government and is present in the funding formulae of the other UK Funding Councils.

A key feature of the Dual Support System, and the award of QR income, for institutions is that the money is not hypothecated. Institutions are free to use the funding to support research however they wish, (although interestingly most universities allocate the funding to departments in a way that mirrors the allocation from HEFCE). It also provides some degree of predictability of funding from one year to the next, which helps forward planning. According to the Government's Science and Innovation Investment Framework: Next Steps report (HM Treasury 2006), the provision of QR allows universities to take strategic decisions about their research activities; builds capacity to undertake 'blue skies' research and research that is not supported from other sources; creates flexibility to react quickly to emerging priorities and new fields of enquiry; and provides a base from which to compete for research funding from other sources. In a nutshell, QR enables stability and underpins innovation. The plans of the Research Councils (and other funders) can achieve their best effects through the Dual Support System as they can build on a foundation put in place as a result of QR funding.

As several commentators have remarked, the Dual Support System and the

Government's commitment to reward excellence through both sides of the system, are key strengths of the UK's science base and have helped to deliver the UK's world class standing in outputs. The key point is that, by international standards, the UK has a higher education system that enjoys a high degree of autonomy in its internal funding decisions and has historically taken advantage of this to make effective early investments in new approaches and fields and to exploit established strengths, which have given the UK its competitive advantage.

Having said this, there is still some ambiguity about the exact scope and purpose of the Funding Council component of the Dual Support System which has evolved over time (Adams and Bekhradnia 2004). Originally it was conceived of in large part to support blue skies research, but it is now increasingly seen largely as providing the basic research infrastructure which underpins institutions' ability to carry out research funded by others. Nevertheless, particularly in the humanities and social sciences, QR income continues to provide the means by which some basic research can be conducted.

The need for reform

In order for the Dual Support System to support research effectively, the Research Council and Funding Council strands need to be relatively balanced. However, since the mid-1980s, this is increasingly not the case. While both the Research Council and Funding Council strands have increased in value, the latter has done so considerably more slowly. Over the period 1980–2000, the ratio of the Funding Council to Research Council part has changed from about 2:1 to 0.5:1 (Adams and Bekradnia 2004). Moreover, as noted by Adams and Bekhradnia, funders of research grants (such as the Research Councils, charities and industry) have behaved like classic purchasers and have sought to maximize the number of grants that they obtain with their money, and universities (and academics within them) have sought an increasing number of grants, because this has been the only way to get more resources. The result has been that more and more project grants are being loaded onto an inadequate research base, and the consequence is in part a decline in the ability of academics to conduct blue skies research, and in part a running down of research infrastructure. National studies of university infrastructure, undertaken in 2001, showed that there was already a very significant backlog in terms of investment required. A report produced by the Office of Science and Technology in 2004 stated that the UK university research system was calculated to be in huge deficit, totalling approximately £1 billion per year (OST 2004). This situation is not unique to the UK. A similar issue of sustainability (or lack of it) has been raised in relation to Australian universities, with their being cited as being around A$900 million out of pocket (THE 2008). In terms of the UK, it is clear that institutions need to be investing more funding on supporting infrastructure, on an annual basis, but few have had the means to develop and finance such a strategy. As a result, the Government has been working with others on a programme to build and maintain a sustainable research base. There are four strands to this reform of the Dual Support System:

- a substantial increase in research funding on both sides of the Dual Support System;
- the introduction of Transparent Approach to Costing (TRAC) methodology to help institutions to calculate the full economic cost of the research work they do, and to understand how these costs are to be met;
- an increasing proportion of the full economic costs of research projects paid by the Research Councils (with a goal of reaching 100 per cent by 2015);
- additional funding to redress the backlog in infrastructure maintenance through the Science Research Infrastructure Scheme (SRIF) and now the Research Capital Investment Fund (RCIF).

In addition, the Government has committed to continue to provide funding on an ongoing basis (as part of their QR income) to help institutions undertake work commissioned by research charities.

TRAC and the move to full economic costing

The Government's 1998 spending review granted additional funds for higher education, but required transparent costing by institutions. The Joint Costing and Pricing Steering Group (JCPSG) was given the task of introducing satisfactory costing methods. The group recommended the implementation of TRAC, a light touch costing methodology, which is based on calculating the costs of different types of academic activity, rather than simply reflecting expenditure (see Chapter 9). As far as research is concerned, implementation of TRAC showed that all research was underfunded when the full economic costs were calculated. The 2002 Government spending review allocated additional funding for research, both in QR and through the Research Councils, and as capital through the SRIF (see below). This funding was awarded on the basis that institutions were required to take responsibility for their own financial sustainability, particularly in respect of research infrastructure. From 2006, it was a requirement that institutions had to apply for Research Council grants on a full economic costing (fEC) basis. The Research Councils pay an agreed proportion of the full economic costs (currently 80 per cent), with institutions making up the balance through QR and other sources. Other funders pay different proportions of the full economic cost, and it is up to institutions to develop a pricing policy to cover this (see Chapter 9).

According to Government, an institution is being managed on a sustainable basis if, taking one year with another, it is recovering the full economic costs across its activities as a whole, and is investing in its infrastructure (physical, human and intellectual), at an appropriate rate. According to the TRAC guidance manual, HEIs need to do five things to manage their research on a sustainable basis. These are:

- establish and recognize the full economic cost of research;
- manage the research activity strategically;
- secure better prices for research;
- improve project management and cost recovery;
- invest in research infrastructure.

Some of these topics are discussed further in Chapter 9.

Capital funding for research

In the UK at least, many universities receive separate allocations of funding to support the building and/or refurbishment of research buildings, major pieces of equipment and so on. A Joint Infrastructure Fund (JIF) was established in the late 1990s, and awarded a total of £750 million to support science research infrastructure projects at 40 UK institutions between 1999 and 2001. The funding was provided by UK government and the Wellcome Trust, and awards were made on a competitive basis. JIF was subsequently replaced by SRIF. This was set up as a joint initiative by the Office of Science and Innovation and the former Department for Education and Skills. It was a UK-wide scheme and its purpose was to contribute to higher education institutions' long-term sustainable research strategies and address past under-investment in research infrastructure (estimated to be approximately £8 billion across the whole UK Higher Education research infrastructure in 2001). SRIF allocated £3 billion to institutions over the period 2002/3 to 2007/8, with the level of funding determined by the level of QR income and the amount of external grant income. In order to assess the success, or otherwise, of SRIF, the Government commissioned an independent report by JM Consulting (HEFCE 2006) to determine how much progress had been made by institutions towards a sustainable infrastructure, and to identify the amount of remedial and recurrent investment that would still be needed. The report drew on evidence from 24 case study institutions across the UK. It concluded that SRIF has been very successful in that it has facilitated an enormous improvement in research infrastructure, halving the backlog since 2001. However, it also concluded that there was still a need for ongoing public investment in research (and teaching) infrastructure and that institutions would still need to receive formulaic funding allocations for this after 2008. The Government has responded by setting up a new UK-wide RCIF, starting in July 2008. The amount of funding going into this is smaller than previously under SRIF as institutions are expected to contribute more towards their own infrastructure costs as a result of the introduction of full economic costing. Allocations are made to institutions in proportion to their level of research income from the UK Research Councils. In addition, institutions can apply for competitively awarded capital funding through schemes such as the joint Wellcome Trust–Wolfson Foundation Capital Funding for Science Based Activities programme (see Chapter 4).

The importance of gaining external funding for research

We have seen why it is important for universities to gain external funding for research, to supplement and, in some countries, influence the amount of unrestricted funding that they get from Government and other sources (for example, by being taken into account in assessment of institutions' performance in exercises such as the RAE and, in future, the Research Excellence Framework). However, even for institutions that perform well in such exercises, there is not enough unrestricted funding to support the range of research activities that universities want, and need, to conduct. Gaining research income is also becoming increasingly important for institutions, as bodies such as the UK Research Councils are starting to award funding to support postgraduate research students on the basis of the amount of grant income won from that Council.

Individual researchers within universities can clearly contribute to the overall corporate goal to increase external research income but, in addition, they will usually have personal motivations for gaining external funding to support their research. Kenway, Boden and Epstein (2007) note five reasons why it is important for researchers to gain external funding. These are because gaining income should:

- enable researchers to broaden and deepen their research work to enhance their research area and career;
- lead to prestigious publications;
- free some time from doing some of the more tedious aspects of university work so they can concentrate more on research;
- enable them to survive in the new performance culture in universities;
- win prestige for the university and for themselves and help them gain promotion and other career enhancements.

In general, gaining external research income makes researchers more productive in that the funding can be spent in several different ways to suit the needs of the researcher and the goals of the project. For example, funding can be used to support the salary of research assistants and other staff who can carry out laboratory experiments, recruit participant populations, gather and analyse data, interrogate specialist collections, analyse texts, and so on; tasks which would be exceedingly time consuming for the researcher. Such staff can also bring expertise that complements that of the grant holder, enabling research questions to be addressed in interesting and appropriate ways. Funding can also be used, with some funding bodies and types of award, to 'buy out' some of the researcher's time from teaching and administration duties, enabling them to spend more of their own time directly on the research project. In addition, some funders allow applicants to request funding to cover the cost of postgraduate research studentships that are directly linked to their proposed projects.

Other ways in which income may be used include buying equipment and other necessary consumables and materials to carry out the project, hosting visiting scholars, setting up research networks, conducting workshops and conferences, and funding travel to support collaborations with researchers based in different institutions and countries. The type and amount of support needed will depend on the nature and aims of the project, and will often be influenced by disciplinary background, as we will see in Chapter 2. However, virtually all types of research will benefit in some way from the provision of external research funding. Similarly, the receipt of external research income will contribute to career advancement for most academic researchers, as it is being increasingly taken into account by selection and promotion committees.

2

Different forms of research and research contexts

Disciplinary differences in research • Collaborative research • Different research settings • Research careers

In order to gain funding for research it is important to know what constitutes 'research' in the eyes of particular funding organizations and where it can be conducted to be eligible for funding. In general, research is about the generation of new knowledge or new applications of knowledge. As noted by Bushaway (2003), the term 'research' was first used in the context of a managed process of systematic investigation or enquiry in the sixteenth century. When the Royal Society was founded in 1660, it was already recognized that research had implications both for the well-being of the national economy and for national security. In the UK, the first government grant for research was given to the Royal Society in 1850. It was not until the mid-twentieth century, however, that there was any significant government funding for research. During the 1950s, basic research was singled out as a key area for public investment not only in the UK but throughout the industrialized world. It is now accepted that research is central to the success of our knowledge-driven economy, creating wealth and employment, underpinning modern public services, informing policy making, developing an understanding of the world around us, and enriching our cultural lives.

There are various different types of research, and they can be classified along a number of different dimensions. It is useful to be familiar with these, and the terminology used to describe them, as you will come across such terms on research funders' websites, etc. In general, basic research (or fundamental research as it is sometimes called) has as its primary objective the advancement of knowledge and theoretical understanding of the relationships among variables. The results of basic research are usually published in scientific journals or research monographs and the primary intended audience is academic peers. Basic research is often driven by researchers' curiosity and is typically conducted with no immediate practical application in mind. This is what most academics immediately think of when it comes to research and, indeed, the opportunity to conduct this type of research is why many of you wanted to become academics. Having said this, there have been many examples over the years of basic research leading to significant and sometimes life changing applications, such as important medical advances and discoveries. For example, a scientist based at Leicester University 'accidentally' discovered DNA fingerprinting while carrying out basic research in his laboratory. There are also examples of basic research having major positive benefits for the economy that would never have been predicted at the time the research was funded. A now classic example is work on game theory, carried out by the ESRC Centre of Economic Learning and Social Evolution at University College London. The Centre was established to undertake basic research in game theory and related areas, but the researchers subsequently persuaded Government to auction third generation mobile phone licences (after devising rules for the exercise) which resulted in the Treasury netting £22.5 billion.

Basic research, particularly scientific research, may be empirically or theoretically motivated. That is, it may start with a question that needs to be addressed, which leads to the design of one or more experiments that will provide the answer and may lead to the development of a theoretical model to account for the data. This in turn may generate new questions and predictions. Alternatively, it can start with a theoretical model or framework that generates questions or predictions that can be tested through experiments, with the outcomes being fed back to refine the models. Whether empirically or theoretically driven, most of the major research funders will want to see how any proposed research fits into a broader theoretical context. Other broad types of basic research include historical research, doctrinal research and research through practice. These in turn involve a range of different methodologies, including experiments, interviews and surveys, modelling and simulations, case studies, ethnography, textual analysis and action research.

Interestingly, there does not seem to be a clearly agreed definition of basic research. Calvert (2004) carried out an empirical study to identify definitions of basic research. The project involved conducting 49 interviews with British and American scientists who carry out 'basic research' and with British and American policy makers who use the expression in their day to day work. The findings showed that most scientists and administrators do not have one all-encompassing idea of 'basic research' but rather draw on many different attributes when defining the term. Calvert concluded that it may be helpful to think of the concept not in terms of one definition, but as having flexible boundaries and multiple dimensions.

Other dimensions that you may well come across distinguish between basic, strategic, applied and contract research. Pure basic research is carried out for the advancement of knowledge, without looking for longer term economic or social benefits, and with no positive efforts being made to apply the findings to practical problems or to transfer the research to sectors responsible for its application. Although still possible, it is becoming increasingly difficult to obtain funding to support pure basic research that has no actual or potential economic, social or cultural impact. Strategic (sometimes called oriented basic) research tends to evolve from basic research. Potential practical applications are feasible and may be likely, but cannot yet be specified. The research is carried out with the expectation that it will produce a broad base of knowledge likely to form the background to the solution of recognized or expected current or future problems. In contrast, applied research is primarily directed towards specified practical aims or objectives, although it will still often involve original investigation in order to acquire new knowledge (OECD 2002). Applied research tends to be more 'short term' in focus and have more immediate ramifications than basic research. To put this more concretely, a series of experiments on visual attention, investigating the effect of distracters in the visual field, conducted solely to inform the development of models of visual attention, would be classified as pure basic research, while carrying out the same studies in the context of driving, with the aim of informing the development of appropriate training systems for drivers, would be considered to be strategic or oriented basic research. Taking the project further to developing a computer based system to allow train drivers to pick up on and respond appropriately to potential hazards in the visual field while driving would count as applied research. Box 2.1 shows the assessment criteria that the UK's Medical Research Council uses in determining whether proposed research should be considered to be basic or applied.

Box 2.1 Assessment criteria used by the UK's Medical Research Council in determining the category of proposed research

Basic Research

- The outcome of the proposed work has many potential applications to a range of needs, processes or products, and/or
- The results of the proposed work will provide significant insights into the mechanism of the targeted illness/condition, which might enable the development of alternative means of managing this illness/condition

Applied Research

- The outcome of the proposed work has a limited range of applications focusing on specific needs and market opportunities, and/or

- The results of the proposed work are mainly restricted to determining the feasibility or otherwise of the proposed product/solution
- Applied projects, although pre-competitive, would be nearer to market than basic ones, with greater medium-term potential benefit to industry
- An important criterion is the extent to which the research will be exploitable, with the most appropriate method for exploitation varying from one industrial sector to another and for different kinds of project

Finally, contract research in universities tends to be undertaken for a third party, external to the university, where both the research to be conducted and the level of payment for it are set out in some form of contract. This contract binds the university to carry out the required work in accordance with a clear specification, a required timescale, and to agreed standards. Contract research is usually driven by the third party's requirements and the results are frequently 'owned' by the third party, restricting the academic freedom of the research team and leaving them little room for manoeuvre (see Chapter 10). Examples of contract research would include evaluating the functionality of a specific piece of software, or the effectiveness of a certain policy, or running a batch of samples through a routine series of tests. As we will see in Chapter 4, universities engage in contract research with a range of different parties including government departments, industry, the EU and the voluntary sector. An issue for many researchers when considering carrying out contract research is that it may be less likely to result in high quality research outputs and, indeed, in some cases the publication of such outputs is restricted (see Chapter 10). On the other hand, you may opt for carrying out a small piece of contract research for a company with the hope that it will lead on to subsequent funding to support more fundamental research.

The above types of research can be distinguished in turn from consultancy (although the distinction between consultancy and contract research can be a grey area). Consultancy is a process through which paying customers gain the benefit of expertise and knowledge in order to provide answers to specific problems. Generally, consultants are experts in a particular field and have wide knowledge of the subject matter in question. They typically provide a particular type of knowledge or service for a specified period of time in exchange for a fee or some 'in kind' benefit, resulting in economy for the client. Most consultancies are of a short duration and can be provided to public, private and charity sector organizations. Consultancy work may be carried out by independent consultants or by staff based within universities or other research organizations. Most universities allow (and indeed encourage) academic staff to engage in a certain amount of consultancy activity in any one year, although they may require the academic to share the resulting income with the institution. The extent to which academics engage in consultancy can be a difficult balance; high levels of consultancy can significantly increase private income sources but will usually mean that less time is available for gaining research funding that is more likely to result in high quality research outputs.

Whether a particular piece of work is provided as a consultancy or as a piece of contract research can have implications for other funding streams. In the UK and Australia, for example, contract research is included in the categories of research income that influence the amount of unrestricted government funding that institutions receive. This is not the case for consultancy income, although the latter can influence some 'third stream' funding sources such as the Higher Education Innovation Fund (HEIF) in the UK. Interestingly, UK universities are reporting increases in levels of both contract research and consultancy. HEFCE's Higher Education Business and Community Interaction Survey 2007–8 reported that the amount of contract research income won by English universities had increased by 10 per cent in 2007–8 compared with the previous year, and that consultancy income had increased by 25 per cent in the same period (HEFCE 2009).

There is also a grey area in terms of whether a piece of work is considered to be research, audit or service evaluation (Smith 1992). In the area of medicine, for example, many studies are classified as audit or service evaluation as opposed to research. In general, clinical audit is a quality improvement process that seeks to improve patient care and outcomes through systematic review of care against explicit criteria and the implementation of change. Thus, there is no search for new knowledge. Rather, performance is reviewed to ensure that what should be done is, in fact, being done. If this is not the case, the audit process should provide a framework to enable improvements to be made. In contrast to audit, service evaluation is designed and conducted solely to define or judge current care, rather than to inform the delivery of best care.

Disciplinary differences in research

While there are commonalities across all types of research, there are some broad differences between the nature of research carried out within particular disciplines. As we will see in the next chapter, research funders such as the UK Research Councils have established a number of different funding schemes and mechanisms to accommodate these different disciplinary traditions.

Within the sciences, much of the research that is carried out follows the scientific method. It provides scientific information and theories for the explanation of the nature and properties of the world around us, and makes practical applications possible. Methods used will vary depending on the subject area but can include observing and measuring human or animal behaviour, interviews and questionnaires, assessing various bodily states, developing and testing new chemical compounds, developing and running simulations and models, and carrying out meta-analyses (where the results of a large number of individual studies are combined to determine overall effect sizes).

When formulating research grant proposals, many scientists will apply for funding to support dedicated research staff and (in some cases) technical and clerical staff, who will carry out much of the day to day work on the project under the direction of the project leader. In many cases the research assistants will join larger research teams working on a set of related projects. Other typical uses of funding will be to pay for equipment and other necessary consumables, or to fund time on large national/international research facilities, such as synchrotron radiation sources, large lasers and telescopes and high performance computers. Not all scientific research is carried out on this scale however. Some scientists, for example pure mathematicians, often have styles of working that are more similar to those of researchers in the arts and humanities, working as lone scholars and not requiring major amounts of funding to support their research. The main need is to be able to free up a sufficient amount of their own time to devote to the research.

Research in the social sciences, and arts and humanities to some extent, shares some of the same methodologies used in scientific research but also involves different traditions, approaches and methods. In addition to the use of interviews, questionnaires, case studies, modelling and (sometimes) experiments, social scientists may also use ethnographic methods (for example, using fieldwork to provide a descriptive study of human societies), as well as different forms of textual or broader communication analyses. Much of the work will require dedicated funding to support research assistants and, sometimes, clerical staff, and pay for materials and other consumables. Other social scientists, however, will work as lone scholars, primarily needing funding to free up their own time to devote to research.

The proportion of researchers who work as lone scholars grows further when one considers arts and humanities research and, as we will see in the next chapter, the Arts and Humanities Research Council (AHRC) has dedicated funding streams to support such working. Increasingly, however, many arts and humanities researchers are working in larger teams to address larger scale projects, often in collaboration with researchers from other disciplines. While arts and humanities researchers use some of the same research approaches and methodologies as social scientists, their focus may be different. For example, while social scientists primarily use content analysis to analyse recorded transcripts or interviews with participants, within the arts and humanities it is more often used to study texts in order to determine meaning, verify authenticity, and so on. Arts and humanities researchers also use other approaches and methodologies that are more associated with their own discipline. These include historical research, doctrinal research, and practice-based or practice-led research.

Collaborative research

In past years, there has been a tendency within institutions to carry out research within specific disciplines. Some academics argue that this tendency has been reinforced by the way in which the RAE and similar exercises primarily assess research at a single discipline level. Increasingly, however, it is being recognized that solution of today's most pressing research problems will require inputs from multidisciplinary teams of researchers, bringing a range of different perspectives, expertise and methodological approaches to address the problem.

Multidisciplinary research can broadly be defined as research which brings together two or more single disciplines in a collaborative way, but draws on research from the core of those disciplines (Bushaway 2003). The term is often used interchangeably with terms such as interdisciplinary research and cross-disciplinary and trans-disciplinary research. There are subtle differences, however, between the meanings of these different terms. Thus, interdisciplinary research tends to be research that is carried out at the interface between two or more single disciplines in a collaborative way, while cross-disciplinary or trans-disciplinary research tends to be research which applies the findings or techniques from one or more disciplines to another (Bushaway 2003). According to Kenway et al. (2007), a multidisciplinary research team is made up of people from different disciplines or professions who are engaged in working together to address a common challenge. The members have to learn to work across disciplines and to share a common vocabulary. In contrast, an interdisciplinary research team is made up of people from multiple disciplines or professions who are engaged in creating and applying new knowledge as they work together as equal stakeholders to address a common challenge. Team members have to have the interactional expertise to work across multiple disciplines as well as within the new interdisciplinary area (Kenway et al. 2007). Similarly, Lowe and Philipson (2006) argue that interdisciplinary research differs from multidisciplinary research in the emphasis that it puts on interaction and joint working, which brings the knowledge claims and conventions of different disciplines into a dialogue with each other, yielding new frameworks of research problems.

The UK Government's Science and Innovation Framework (2004–14) stresses the need to enhance a culture of multidisciplinary (although they probably meant interdisciplinary as well) research in the UK, and provide the underpinning infrastructure and funding mechanisms to support it (HM Treasury 2004). In line with this, the UK Research Councils (and other funders) have been increasingly promoting the importance of, and need for, multidisciplinary and interdisciplinary research. According to the Research Council's UK website, novel multidisciplinary approaches are needed to solve many, if not all, of the biggest research challenges over the next 10 to 20 years. Such challenges include how the brain works and how its understanding will lead to new forms of computing; whether we can predict rapid climate change and its impacts; how the UK will cope with an increasingly ageing population; and how to manage increasing demands for energy and other natural resources. Research Councils UK (RCUK) have put in place a broad portfolio of funding mechanisms to support such working, including funding large multidisciplinary and interdisciplinary research centres within universities. As set out in its latest delivery plan, RCUK is currently supporting six large multidisciplinary research programmes, each of which involves several of the individual Research Councils (RCUK 2007a). These programmes are: living with environmental change; energy; global uncertainties – security for all in a changing world; ageing – lifelong health and well-being; digital economy; and nanoscience through engineering to application (see Chapter 3). The total amount of funding allocated to support research in these priority areas is nearly £1400 million.

The growing recognition of the importance of multidisciplinary and interdisciplinary research, and its promotion and dedicated funding by the Research Councils, has also led many universities to form new horizontally organized research structures, cutting across individual disciplinary based departments. A brief tour through university web pages will show that a large number of new multidisciplinary and interdisciplinary research centres and institutes have been established since the mid-2000s. These centres bring researchers from different disciplines together, in either a physical or virtual way.

Despite the encouragement from both research funders and from universities themselves for staff to engage in multidisciplinary and interdisciplinary working, some researchers have preferred to keep working at a single discipline level. This may be because they want to keep control over, and ownership of, their own research, and are concerned about some of the additional tensions that collaborative working across disciplines can bring. They may also be concerned about the additional time it can take to develop good working relationships, a shared language and understanding, and fundable proposals and manageable projects. Boucher et al. (2004) note that, although universities are in principle supportive of multidisciplinary and interdisciplinary working, they still have internal management and resourcing processes that operate on a more disciplinary/traditional department basis, and this may make multidisciplinary working even more challenging. As collaborative projects progress, problems can arise over partners not delivering their share of the work according to agreed timescales, authorship of publications and ownership of any intellectual property that arises from the project. In general, you should not engage in multidisciplinary collaborative projects simply for the sake of it. The nature of the research should drive the formation of an appropriately qualified research team. There should be a clear reason why each person is a member of the team and what they can contribute to and gain from the research.

Different research settings

Many people reading this book will be researchers based within universities. Most 'permanent' academic staff in universities are employed on contracts that cover both teaching and research. However, some are employed in a teaching-only or research-only capacity. Across the sector, relatively few staff employed in lecturer, senior lecturer, reader or professorial roles have research-only contracts. Such contracts are primarily given to research assistants, fellows and more senior research staff, who may be employed on either a fixed term or 'permanent' basis. The type of contract on which you are employed will determine the extent to which your institution supports you to carry out research and your eligibility to apply for certain external funding schemes.

In many universities, academic staff will be provided with the basic environmental infrastructure to support research, including library and IT services, and some are given some allowance for spending time on research. In other universities, however, this does not come as a right, and academics are only able to carry out research if they have external (or sometimes internal) funding to cover the time spent away from teaching and other academic duties. Many universities will also have in place an environment that is supportive of research. This will involve things like regular research seminars by internal or visiting staff, hosting visiting research scholars on a longer term basis, access to larger research equipment and other facilities, dedicated technicians and administrative staff, and dedicated research development offices. These offices employ staff to help researchers seek out and apply for external research funding, negotiate and draw up contracts and manage research accounts. In larger, more research intensive, universities, such staff may also be employed within particular departments or units, enabling them to provide a more tailored service.

As we have seen above, in some disciplinary areas researchers have traditionally been able to conduct their research, at least to a certain degree, without gaining any, or any large amounts of, external research funding. They are typically provided with the basic support needed to carry out desk based research, and will only require additional funding if their other work commitments prevent them from being able to devote sufficient time to research. Even in these disciplines, however, there is an increasing shift towards encouraging staff to gain some level of external funding to support their research. In other cases, however, particularly within the sciences, research simply cannot be conducted without some dedicated external (although sometimes internal) funding to support research staff, equipment, materials and so on. Researchers do not have the time, resources and sometimes the range of expertise that is needed to carry out serious research projects. Many universities do undertake to support new early career researchers who work in such areas until they are in a position to gain external funding for themselves (see Chapter 6). However, they are usually only able to do this for a relatively limited time period.

As noted in Chapter 1, research in universities has largely ceased to be a 'private matter' for individual academics. Most are given clear expectations about the extent to which they are, or are not, expected to engage in research (and will be supported to do so). Partly as a result of exercises such as the UK's RAE, universities have put in place much more formal research planning and management mechanisms. Academic staff who are expected to engage in research may have to produce periodic research plans and reports so that their performance can be assessed and evaluated in some way. The performance of departments and other units is, in turn, monitored by more senior management, and the allocation of future resources may depend on how well such units are performing (see Chapter 10). Despite this increased level of management within universities, many academic staff still have considerable freedom about what type of research they choose to conduct and the particular projects they work on. There may be some encouragement to work with particular groups or on work related to selected research themes, but there is usually a fair degree of freedom. In many other research settings this is often not the case, with staff being employed to work on specific projects or in specific research areas. However, even within universities, researchers do not have complete freedom over choice of funding source. Most universities operate policies that do not normally allow their staff to apply for funding from certain funding sectors, such as organizations associated with the tobacco industry. Similarly, university management might not accept funding contracts from organizations that will not pay for the full economic cost of the research, if supporting the research in question is not in the strategic interest of the university (see Chapter 9).

The majority of research in the UK, and probably throughout the industrialized world, is not carried out in universities but is conducted within industry, business, government departments, or dedicated research institute settings. Industry and business not only fund, but also carry out, the greatest proportion of research in the UK, more than three times that carried out by Higher Education Institutes (Bushaway 2003). Researchers working within these settings usually have less academic freedom than those working within a university setting (unless in the latter case they are employed as a member of research staff relating to a specific project or programme). Although industries and businesses fund and carry out some blue skies research, much of what they do is understandably much closer to market. Researchers will often be linked to one or more specific research and development project. Researchers working within government departments will also often be linked to specific research programmes, working on policy related questions. Much of the work is likely to involve the evaluation of the success, or otherwise, of particular policies and schemes. Clearly, some work within the National Health Service (NHS) is of this nature, although much of the research that is carried out within hospitals and Primary Care Trusts will have a more clinical focus and, in some cases, may not differ that much in approach from research conducted within universities. Irrespective of the nature of the research concerned, staff working within NHS Trusts can only carry out research within the Trust if they obtain research and development (R&D) management approval for the research in question. The R&D management office will want to reassure themselves that there is either external funding to support the research or that the level of resources required to carry out the project (including the researcher's time) is such that it could be 'covered' by the Trust.

Most industrialized countries also have a number of large dedicated research institutes, many of which will be funded by government. Many of these units will have been established to address research in particular areas, such as agriculture or food research, or research relating to particular medical conditions. Large units funded by the UK government include the Atomic Weapons Establishment, the Defence Scientific and Technical Laboratory, the Meteorological Office, National Physical Laboratory, and the Central Science Laboratory. Several of the UK Research Councils also sponsor dedicated research units and institutes. The Medical Research Council (MRC), for example, currently funds 28 institutes and three units in the UK (costing over £300 million per year), which carry out research across the biomedical research spectrum, from fundamental science at the molecular level to large scale epidemiological studies. These include the Clinical Trials Unit, Cognition and Brain Sciences Unit, Human Genetics Unit, and the Social and Public Health Services Unit. The Biotechnology and Biological Sciences Research Council (BBSRC) also sponsors dedicated research institutes that conduct long term, mission oriented, research using specialized facilities. Currently supported units include the John Innes Centre and Rothampsted Research (both focused on sustainable agriculture and land use), the Institute for Animal Health and the Babraham Institute and Institute of Food Research. Other Research Council supported institutes and large research facilities include the Centre for Ecology and Hydrology, the UK Astronomy Centre and the Daresbury and Rutherford Appleton Laboratories. Staff working in such institutes are often restricted in terms of the types of research in which they can engage and their eligibility to apply for external funding.

Research careers

As noted above, many of you reading this book will be based within universities or other HEIs. The majority will be employed in academic positions, involving a combination of teaching, research and administration. Most such academics enter the system at the lecturer level and then, if progression occurs, move on through a senior lectureship and/or readership position, to a professorship. A smaller proportion is employed either on teaching-only or research-only contracts. The majority of academics have 'permanent' contracts but a number are employed on a fixed term basis, for example for three or five years. As noted in Chapter 1, gaining external research income is now an important component of career progression for most academics, being increasingly taken into account by appointment, probationary review and promotion panels.

Universities also employ large numbers of researchers, often as research assistants or fellows on fixed-term contracts, who are normally attached to specific research projects. Some of these will move on to obtain academic lectureships in due course, but others will leave academia and take up employment in other sectors. Researchers who have gained some independent external grant income or substantially contribute to the development of proposals of more senior investigators are likely to be more successful at moving on to academic positions, particularly in the sciences. Holding a short-term research assistantship or fellowship can be an uncertain time career-wise, particularly when researchers have been employed on a number of successive short-term contracts. Such researchers are often constrained in terms of not being able to apply for many types of funding in their own name, and are often restricted in their ability to take on long-term financial commitments, such as mortgages. There is now European legislation which restricts the overall length of time staff can be employed on continuous short-term contracts, but issues still remain.

Concerns over difficulties faced by 'contract research staff' led to a Research Careers Initiative in the UK, which produced a Concordat on contract research staff, agreed by major funding organizations, such as the Research Councils, Royal Society and British Academy and Universities UK. The original version was published in 1996, with a revised version in 2008 (www.researchconcordat.ac.uk). The purpose of the Concordat is to improve the terms and conditions of employment, quality of career guidance and personal and career development opportunities for contract research staff (see Chapter 10).

As mentioned above, in addition to working in HEIs, a number of researchers will be employed within government-funded research institutes, independent research organizations, government departments, and private sector organizations. Some of these will be employed on fixed-term contracts but a good number will be employed in 'permanent' positions, working on a series of projects over the course of their employment. Most organizations that employ such researchers have developed clear career structures to enable development and career progression.

3

Who funds research?
Part 1: the UK Research Councils

*The UK Research Councils • Research Council Delivery Plans
(2008–2011) • New emerging themes • Different modes of funding
and forms of support • Success rates*

An important first step in gaining funding for research is to know about potential funding sources so that you can target the most appropriate organization.
A large number of public and private organizations provide funding for
research. Around £14 billion is spent each year supporting research in the UK,
by a combination of public bodies, private enterprise, the non-profit sector
and international organizations. This does not mean however that you will
find it easy to access such funding. Most organizations that provide funding
have very specific ideas about what they want to spend their money on, either
in terms of research areas addressed or types of support they want to provide.
This chapter and the following one outline the main bodies that provide
funding for research, and the types of funding schemes that are available,
for UK based researchers. Clearly some of these schemes will also be open
to researchers from other countries. Chapter 3 focuses on the UK Research
Councils, which are Government funded bodies that support research in all
areas of science, engineering, technology, social science, arts and humanities.
Most other countries in the developed world have established, or are establishing, similar bodies. Research Council funding is often seen as the most prestigious type of funding and many academics strive to gain Research Council
awards. However, there are many other sources of funding and, accordingly,
Chapter 4 looks at a number of other funding bodies, including research charities, professional associations, industry, and the European Union. The aim of

these chapters is to provide you with information about the main research funding organizations and the various schemes they support. Advice on what they are looking for when funding proposals, and how to increase your chances of gaining an award is presented in later chapters. You will probably not need, or want, to read exhaustively through the present chapter and the next. Rather you should simply skip through the various sections picking up on funding sources and schemes that are potentially relevant for you.

The UK Research Councils

As we saw in Chapter 1, the UK Research Councils form one strand of the UK's Dual Support System. Their primary role is to fund research, and this is mostly done on a competitive basis. Each year the councils, jointly, invest around £1.3 billion in research in UK universities, around £500 million in their own research institutes and around £300 million in access to international facilities for UK researchers. Collectively they support around 18000 grants and 50000 researchers at any one time. Together the Research Councils cover the full range of academic disciplines, from the medical and biological sciences, the engineering and physical sciences, to the social sciences and arts and humanities. The research ranges from fundamental blue skies investigation, through longer term strategic research, to more applied research activities. Increasingly they have to demonstrate the broader economic, social and cultural impact of the research they fund in order to justify their funding from Government. All of the Research Councils have strong user representation on their governing councils and advisory bodies, and most have specific user advisory panels. The Research Councils vary in size and budget, ranging from just over £100 million a year (in the case of the Arts and Humanities Research Council) to over £800 million per year (in the case of the Engineering and Physical Sciences Research Council – EPSRC). The broad research remits of the different councils tend to remain pretty steady over the years, but within the broad area of their coverage they are likely to change their focus and priorities every few years.

In many cases it is a routine decision as to which particular council is appropriate for supporting your research. In some areas, however, it might be less clear and you may need to think more carefully about how to 'frame' particular projects depending on the different emphases and priorities of the different councils. If the main aim of your research is to understand how the human brain works, for example, BBSRC would be appropriate, whereas if the main aim is to improve human health and well-being then MRC would be better. Similarly, if the main purpose is to understand visual processing in partially sighted individuals then BBSRC, or possibly MRC, might be appropriate, whereas if the aim is to improve the design of buildings so that partially sighted individuals can navigate around them more easily then EPSRC would be better. It is important to frame your proposed research in a way that is appropriate for the targeted council. Not doing so can lead to your project being passed from one council to another, which can slow down the assessment process, or, even worse, to you receiving low ratings from reviewers and assessors.

The following sections provide a very brief summary of the main remits of each of the councils. More detailed information can be found on their websites.

Biotechnology and Biological Sciences Research Council

The BBSRC was established in 1994 by merging the former Agricultural and Food Research Council with the Biotechnology and Biological Science Programmes from the former Science and Engineering Research Council (SERC). Its current annual budget is around £450 million a year. BBSRC funds research in plants, microbes and animals (including humans), from the level of molecules and cells, to tissues, whole organisms, populations and landscapes, as well as funding development of the tools and technology underpinning biological research. Specific areas covered include:

- genomics, stem biology, and bio-nanotechnology, that provide a basis for new technologies in healthcare, food safety, plant and livestock breeding and bio-processing;
- whole organism biology relevant to the understanding of diet and health, ageing, animal health and welfare, infectious diseases and immunity and crop productivity;
- biological populations and systems that underpin agricultural sustainability, biodiversity and novel bio-based and renewable processes for energy and manufacturing.

BBSRC does not fund research that is focused on specific human diseases and disease processes or abnormal conditions, which fall within the remit of the MRC, nor does it fund studies primarily involving animal models of human disease and human toxicology, including abnormal toxicological reactions.

Over one-third of BBSRC's research budget is spent on supporting responsive mode (open competition) research grants each year, with around another third supporting core strategic grants and other research initiatives.

Medical Research Council

The MRC has a long history, with its origins stemming from the 1911 National Insurance Act and the establishment of the Medical Research Committee and Advisory Council in 1913. The MRC's mission is to improve human health through world class medical research, and it supports research across the biomedical spectrum from fundamental laboratory based science to clinical trials in all major disease areas. It works closely with the NHS and UK health departments. Its remit covers

- the use of animals in research;
- antibiotic resistance;
- brain sciences;
- genomics and proteomics;
- public health;
- intensive care;
- patient safety research;
- stem cell research.

Current priority areas include clinical and public health research, infections and vaccines research, global health, biomarkers, and age-related research. The MRC's annual budget is around £650 million, with more than half of this supporting its research units and institutes.

Engineering and Physical Sciences Research Council

The EPSRC was also formed in 1994, taking over much of the original SERC portfolio. It is the largest of the Research Councils and is the main UK government agency for funding research and training in engineering and physical sciences, investing around £810 million a year, with around £500 million of this supporting research grants. Specific areas of research covered in its remit include:

- mathematics, chemistry, and physics;
- materials science;
- engineering and computer science;
- energy research;
- information and communications technology;
- research into the built environment;
- research into innovative manufacturing.

Natural Environment Research Council

The NERC funds environmental research, survey and observation work. It was founded in 1965 by drawing together a variety of environmental research organizations and surveys, including the Nature Conservancy, the Geological Survey of Great Britain, the National Institute of Oceanography and the Hydrological Research Unit and British Antarctic Survey. Its work covers the full range of atmospheric, earth, biological, terrestrial and aquatic sciences, from the deep oceans to the upper atmosphere, and from the poles to the equator. NERC's current budget is around £400 million a year. Specific areas covered in its remit include:

- the geo- and earth sciences, hydrology, soil science, atmospheric research and oceanography;
- biological and microbiological research on animal and plant biodiversity, population dynamics and ecology;
- climate change research;
- environmental chemistry and physics;
- satellite based Earth observation;
- polar research;
- management of land and natural resources.

Almost half of NERC's annual budget is spent on supporting national capability in terms of funding essential infrastructure and facilities for the environmental sciences, including a number of large centres and national surveys. Between 20 and 25 per cent is spent on both directed programmes and responsive mode grants, with the majority of this being used to support research on earth systems science, climate systems and biodiversity.

Economic and Social Research Council

The ESRC began in 1965 as the Social Science Research Council. Following the Rothschild Review, which recommended a greater focus on empirical research and research related to public concerns, the Council was restructured in 1983 under the new name of Economic and Social Research Council. The Council funds social science and economic research across a wide range of disciplines encompassing sociology, economics, anthropology, political science, area or regionally based research and geography, international relations, cultural and media studies, law and linguistics and psychology. Areas currently being addressed, as set out in its 2009–2014 Strategic Plan (ESRC 2009) include

- understanding behaviour;
- technology and innovation;
- environment and energy;
- security and conflict;
- social diversity;
- global economy.

ESRC's annual budget is around £180 million, with over £100 million of this supporting research centres, programmes, grants, fellowships and resources.

Arts and Humanities Research Council

The AHRC was established in 2005, having evolved from the Arts and Humanities Research Board. AHRC supports arts and humanities research that furthers our understanding of human culture and creativity, spanning a wide range from ancient history and heritage science to modern dance and digital content. It covers traditional humanities subjects such as history, archaeology, English, linguistics, law, modern languages, philosophy and classics and inter-disciplinary studies, as well as the creative and performing arts. In addition to supporting research grants, fellowships and research leave across these areas, it also currently funds three large initiatives in Religion and Society, Science and Heritage, and Beyond Text. AHRC's annual budget is just over £100 million, with around half of this directly supporting research awards.

Science and Technology Facilities Council

Finally, the STFC is the newest of the Research Councils. It was formed in 2007 through a merger of the Council for the Central Laboratory of the Research Councils (CCLRC) and the Particle and Physics and Astronomy Research Council (PPSRC), and the transfer of nuclear physics from the EPSRC. Its cur-rent annual budget is around £630 million a year, and it funds research in universities in astronomy, particle physics, space science and nuclear physics. It also provides UK access to large scale research facilities such as the Synchro-tron Radiation Source, the Central Laser Facility, ISIS, and the High Perform-ance Computing Centre, as well as a number of major facilities overseas, such as the European Space Agency.

Research Council Delivery Plans (2008–2011)

As outlined in Chapter 1, the Research Councils get their funding from UK Government. Not surprisingly, they have to make a strong case for this fund-ing and justify how it is spent and, increasingly, what impact the research they fund has. In December 2007, the Research Councils published their latest 'delivery plans', which set out their strategic priority areas for the following three to four year period. Their individual priorities include coverage, where relevant, of the six RCUK targeted multidisciplinary research priority areas – energy; living with environmental change; global uncertainties – security for all in a changing world; ageing – lifelong health and well-being; digital econ-omy; and nanoscience through engineering to application – outlined in the previous chapter. RCUK believes that novel multidisciplinary approaches are needed to solve the important research challenges in these key areas. Several of the councils are involved in each of the six priority programmes. The remit of the different programmes, and the specific councils involved, are shown in Appendix 2. If you are working in one of these broad areas it is worth contact-ing the relevant programme manager to find out what specific funding opportunities exist or are likely to be coming up.

In addition to identifying which of the six multidisciplinary programmes they are contributing to, the individual Research Councils have set out a number of other specific priority areas in their individual 2007–11 delivery plans, as shown in Appendix 3. Some of these priority areas will be carried forward in future delivery plans, but others are likely to change as new priorities emerge.

New emerging themes

In addition to engaging in the six targeted multidisciplinary research programmes, the Research Councils have identified three emerging multidisciplinary priority themes, in which they expect to make some focused investment. These are as follows.

Food Security

It is not surprising that food security has been highlighted as an important emerging theme given the fact that an adequate, safe and secure food supply is a fundamental human need and is essential for political stability and wider economic prosperity. We know that the world will have to double its food supply up to 2050 with very little additional cultivatable land remaining. The research challenge is therefore to maximize sustainable productivity without degrading natural resources, and to do this within a socially and economically wider framework. Development of the theme is being led by BBSRC.

Connected Communities

This second theme focuses on the notion that, in an increasingly interconnected and mobile society, economic prosperity, health, sustainability and well-being will depend on how our connections evolve with each other, with our cultural heritage and with our natural and built environment. Research within this theme will therefore help to exploit the opportunities and tackle the challenges faced by these connected communities. Development of the theme is being led by AHRC.

Fostering Recovery and Enhancing Resilience

Finally, it has become abundantly clear since 2008 that to compete in a global economy and achieve lasting prosperity, the UK economy must insulate itself to be resilient to future shocks. Investment will be made in the UK research and skills base to build long-term manufacturing capability through the application of, and adaptation to, green systems, solutions and technologies. Development of this theme is being led by EPSRC.

At the time of writing it is not yet clear whether or not there will be dedicated funding streams associated with these new priority areas. However, it is very likely that there will be increased opportunities for funding for those of you working in the broad areas covered by these three themes.

Different modes of funding and forms of support

The Research Councils, like a number of other funders, offer a range of different types of support, from providing funding for large research units and centres through to small grants for new researchers. The particular forms of support offered by each of the councils, and details of eligibility and other important information, are outlined in their guides to funding and on their websites. In general, the Research Councils primarily fund research that is based in UK Higher Education Institutions, although some also fund research based in Research Council institutes or independent research organizations (such as the Institute for Fiscal Studies, National Centre for Social Research, Transport Research Laboratory, and various Trusts and museums). As an applicant for Research Council support, you must be resident in the UK at the time of application and, in most cases, hold an appointment which is resourced from central funds of the host institution, and be appointed at lecturer level or equivalent. Most of the councils require applicants to have either a permanent contract of employment or one that is longer than the duration of the proposed research project. However, there are exceptions to these eligibility requirements and it is important to check the specific eligibility criteria for the particular Research Council and scheme in question before you apply.

Research institutes, units and centres

As mentioned in Chapter 2, several of the Research Councils sponsor dedicated research institutes or units employing their own researchers (and other staff). MRC funded units, for example, carry out research across the biomedical research spectrum. Similar establishments are funded by BBSRC, NERC and the STFC. The majority of research carried out by these institutes and units is funded from the core funding allocated to them by their host Council, although research staff based within them are eligible to bid for some external funding schemes.

In addition to these large institutes and units, most of the councils also provide funding for dedicated research centres, usually for a time limited period. These centres are mainly housed within universities, and the expectation is that they will become financially sustainable once the period of core Research Council funding has elapsed. When establishing such centres, one or more Research Council decides that it wants to focus support and build research capacity in a particular research area (often a new and emerging area) and issues a call for proposals. In most cases the original call is for outline proposals, a number of which are then shortlisted, and selected researchers are invited to submit full proposals. To be successful, applications need to show evidence of a strong research team, with appropriate experience and expertise, led by a first class researcher. There also needs to be support from the host university or universities, and there need to be clear plans for carrying out cutting edge research in the area in question. Although competitions for the establishment of such centres are normally open to all researchers, only the strongest of research teams, with the best track records, will stand any chance of success. Unless you meet these criteria, applying for this form of support is a waste of your time and an additional unnecessary load on the peer review system.

Research networks

Some of the Research Councils, as well as other funders, also provide funding for the establishment of (usually multidisciplinary) research networks. The primary aim is to build capacity by creating new research teams, who might not yet have established sufficient track record to succeed with a bid for a new centre. Funding is typically provided for travel, workshops and the like, in order to bring researchers together to advance an area and, sometimes, work on proposals for future research in the area in question. Funding to support research networks is often tied to large time-limited research programmes in areas deemed to be of strategic importance and priority, such as the New Dynamics of Ageing Programme led by ESRC. However, some councils allow researchers to apply for support for research networks in any area within their remit. EPSRC, for example, supports networks where the aim is to create new interdisciplinary research communities and topics, by developing interaction between the research community and appropriate science, technology and industrial groups. The main aims are to transfer experimental techniques, models and scientific insights and to promote mobility between academe, universities and industry. Networks are expected to lead to new collaborative multidisciplinary research proposals, and some may develop into virtual centres of excellence, providing critical mass of analytic expertise. Bids may be submitted at any point during the year and should be for support of up to three years' duration. Similarly, AHRC also provides support for interdisciplinary research workshops and networks. The former awards normally entail the organization of a set of events over a period of one year to bring researchers from a range of disciplines together with other interested parties to explore and develop the research area in question. Awards cover operating and support costs involved in organizing a short term series of interdisciplinary workshops. Interdisciplinary research network awards, in contrast, are intended to allow more extensive interaction between researchers from a range of disciplines and other interested parties than is achievable through a workshop award, in terms of both the number and range of participants and scope of activities that can be supported. Finally, ESRC runs an annual research seminars scheme, which provides support for multidisciplinary groups of academic researchers, post-graduate research students and non-academic units who meet regularly to exchange information and ideas with the aim of advancing research within their fields. They particularly encourage bids designed to bring together leading researchers from across disciplines to identify new research agendas or capacity building priorities. Awards are normally made up to a maximum of £15000. If you are trying to build up a new interdisciplinary team or network then it is worth looking at these various forms of funding as even a relatively small amount of money can help you to test out the strength and potential value of a new collaboration.

Directed and responsive mode funding

Before describing other common modes of support, it is worth distinguishing between directed as opposed to responsive mode funding. All of the Research Councils offer both forms of support, and need to provide for an appropriate balance between the two. Directed funding, as its name suggests, is provided to support research in a particular area. The Research Councils, either alone or jointly, call for proposals for centres, networks, research programmes and grants, or whatever, in a targeted area that is deemed to be of importance for the UK's economic competitiveness and/or quality of life. Thus, research funded under the RCUK's six large multidisciplinary programmes described above, would be examples of the application of directed funding. Responsive mode funding, in contrast, is not tied to specific research areas. You can bid for support for research grants, programmes, or whatever, in any area that falls within the overall remit of the funder in question. Responsive mode funding is rarely used to support new research centres or networks, as these tend to be directed at building research and research capacity in targeted areas. Responsive mode support is more commonly used to fund research grants and programmes, as well as research fellowships and the like. Responsive mode funding has traditionally been aligned with supporting curiosity driven research. However, increasingly such research is expected to have some economic, social or cultural impact (see Chapters 5 and 7).

Research grants and programmes

This is the most common type of support requested by researchers. Most of you will start, or have started, by applying for research grants (often small ones), that allow you to address particular research questions and begin to develop your track record (see Chapter 6). Research grants typically run for one to three years (although occasionally longer) and usually employ one or more research assistants (who in some cases may be the applicant) and other support staff if appropriate. Funding can also be used to purchase dedicated equipment and necessary consumables and materials, buy time on major national and international research facilities, cover the costs of human and animal research participants, gain access to specialist collections and support travel and conference attendance. Some funding schemes will also provide funding for postgraduate research studentships associated with the project. Information about the specific types of support that each council is willing to fund will be available in their individual Guides to Funding. There will also be information about what they will not support. ESRC, for example, states that research grant applications cannot be accepted for:

- unspecified research work;
- research already carried out;
- writing up previous research;
- literature surveys;
- conferences attended, other than with an award;
- travel for general study;
- expeditions;
- unsolicited requests to hold conferences;
- preparation of books and publications;
- preparation and production of curriculum materials and software development.

It is important to know what type of support is provided by a funding organization or through a certain scheme to make sure it is appropriate for your proposed project.

Once you have gained some experience of managing research teams, and producing high quality publications, it may be appropriate to move on to applying for larger programme grants. The MRC states, for example, that programme grants help the medical science community to 'think bigger'. Such programme grants typically last for longer periods of time (often five years) and cover a number of related strands of research, and employ several researchers and other support staff as needed for the type of research in question. This is reflected in the typical size of grant. Most research grants typically fall within the £100 000 to £1 million price range (with the majority being for around £300 000), whereas funding for programme grants will typically be over one million pounds. Thus, they are not an appropriate form of support if you are a new researcher, as you would need to show experience of having successfully managed previous projects before any of the councils would want to commit such a large sum of money.

Rather than have separate research grant and research programme schemes, some Research Councils offer small and large research grants. ESRC, for example, runs a small grants scheme for projects up to £100 000 and a large grants scheme for large scale research projects of up to five years. The types of project that the latter scheme aims to address are those that are beyond the usual scope of ESRC standard grants and which are in the range of £1.5 million to £5 million. BBSRC has also introduced a Longer Larger Awards scheme

(LOLAs). These are responsive mode research grants valued at £2 million or more. Projects must aim to address strategically important biological problems that merit large scale commitments. Again, these larger awards are more appropriate for researchers and research teams who have already built up strong track records. If you are still at a relatively early stage of career you should not apply for such awards unless working in collaboration with more senior researchers. Even then, it would not usually be appropriate for you to be the lead researcher on such a proposal.

Both directed and responsive mode funding are used to support research grants and programmes. In the former case, the funding organization calls for proposals for research grants and programmes within the targeted area of interest, whereas in the latter case researchers are free to apply for support for grants and programmes in any research area within the overall remit of the funding body. Most councils allow applications at any point during the year, although some operate fixed deadlines for certain schemes.

Most of the Research Councils also run dedicated schemes, or special procedures, aimed specifically at new researchers. These are described in Chapter 6.

Research fellowships

The above funding schemes provide support for projects or larger programmes of research. A number of schemes, however, are aimed specifically at supporting individuals rather than projects per se. The main criterion when awarding funding is the strength of the researcher's track record and their future potential. All of the Research Councils provide funding for research fellowships and similar individual based awards. Some offer several types of fellowship award aimed at researchers at different stages of their research career. Whether to apply for a research grant or a fellowship will depend on your personal motivation. Research grant applications tend to be more suited to cases where you have a very specific research project in mind, with a series of research questions that need to be addressed, and that typically require employing one or more research assistants. Fellowship applications, on the other hand, are more appropriate where you want to conduct research in a particular area, but primarily want to progress your own career development. Thus a fellowship application might be suitable at an early stage of career if you are a new postdoctoral researcher who wants a year's support to enable you to develop your ideas to be in a position to apply for more substantial funding. Similarly, at a later career stage, a fellowship application might be appropriate if you are an established academic who needs some time to develop your thinking to 'take your research to the next level'. In most cases, fellowships will be ideally suited to where buying out all, or a substantial proportion, of your time is the number one need.

AHRC, for example, introduced a new Research Fellowships scheme in 2009, to replace its former Research Leave scheme. It is open to early career, mid-career, and senior/professorial candidates. Length of awards varies between three and nine months, and duration needs to be fully justified in terms of the research activities to be undertaken, the expected outputs, and the value added to the institutional support for the Fellow. Award holders must dedicate between 50 per cent and 100 per cent of their time to the fellowship. Funding, up to a maximum of £120 000, is provided to cover the costs of the research and communication and dissemination activities. More detail on the early career fellowships is given in Chapter 6. AHRC also supports research fellowships in the Creative and Performing Arts to support artists as researchers within UK Higher Education Institutions. These fellowships can be held for two to three years full-time or five years part-time.

ESRC offers support for three different levels of fellowship: Postdoctoral, Mid-Career Development, and Professorial Fellowships. The former are aimed at those of you who are at a very early stage of your academic career and show a lot of potential (further information is provided in Chapter 6). The Mid-Career Fellowships are aimed at those of you who have between five and fifteen years' postdoctoral experience, and are intended to enable outstanding researchers to take their research in new directions or to the next level. Finally, the Professorial Fellowships support leading social scientists by providing them with freedom to pursue innovative and creative research agendas. To be successful, you must have an outstanding track record of research and be an acknowledged scholarly leader in your field at an international level.

BBSRC similarly runs a number of fellowship schemes for researchers working within UK Higher Education Institutions. Their David Phillips Fellowships are aimed at relatively early career scientists who have established themselves as independent researchers, and provide funding for five years. To be eligible, you must have between three and ten years' postdoctoral research experience (further information is provided in Chapter 6). In contrast, BBSRC's Professorial Fellowships are aimed at supporting world class scientists who are already recognized at the international level as being outstanding researchers with the potential to use the fellowship to open up dramatic and novel lines of work in UK bioscience. Candidates are expected to be freed of all significant university teaching and administrative commitments, since the fellowship will fund the proportion of the Fellow's time not already committed to research grant projects. BBSRC also fund Research Development Fellowships for scientists seeking to undertake new directions in their research, such as developing interdisciplinary dimensions by integrating new techniques or methodologies. Finally, they fund Returners to Work Fellowships for scientists wanting to return to research after taking a career break. In addition to these four schemes, BBSRC also supports enterprise and industry fellowships. Enterprise Fellowships are aimed at supporting researchers who want to be actively involved in commercializing their own research, whereas Industrial Fellowships are aimed at promoting collaboration between the UK science base and industry by supporting the exchange of mid-career researchers either from the science base to industry or vice-versa.

NERC, EPSRC and MRC also run various types of fellowship scheme aimed at researchers at different stages of career, with the MRC schemes being aimed at either clinical or non-clinical researchers. Further details of current schemes are available on the Councils' websites.

Other schemes

Finally, most of the Research Councils also support a number of other smaller schemes, often aimed at encouraging and facilitating collaborations with international partners or with Government departments (such as the Ministry of Defence) and with business and industry (see Chapter 4). In the former case, BBSRC, for example, runs an International Science Interchange Scheme (ISIS) aimed at facilitating and promoting international collaborations. The purpose of the scheme is to provide a mechanism to initiate and pump-prime collaborations to allow scientists to explore the potential for new linkages to add an international dimension to their BBSRC funded research. Funding is available for travel and subsistence for UK based applicants. BBSRC also provides funding for international workshops, and to enable BBSRC supported research groups to forge long-term relationships with Japanese, Chinese, Indian or American scientists working in areas of direct relevance to BBSRC's current strategic plan. Most of the other Research Councils fund similar schemes. In 2009 ESRC established a scheme specifically to boost international mobility, exchange and networking for early career researchers. Their new International Activities for Early Career Researchers scheme aims to support established international networks and activities, or the development of new activities based upon clear evidence of need or demand (see Chapter 6).

Success rates

Whatever type of grant or fellowship you are considering, it is useful to know something about your likely chances of success. Clearly, the Research Councils only have limited amounts of funding, and are only able to fund the strongest researchers and the most competitive proposals. In order to give researchers some idea of their likely chances of gaining funding, they now routinely publish success rates associated with their different competitions. Since around 2007, success rates for standard research grants have typically been between 20 and 30 per cent. Most Research Councils like to keep their success rates for responsive mode awards at above 25 per cent, but this can be challenging when application rates are high and funding is limited. Data published by the Research Councils in 2009 shows that success rates, across councils, fell from 28 per cent in 2007–8 to 23 per cent in 2008–9. Table 3.1 shows success rates in 2008–9, compared with 2007–8, for each of the councils. More detailed information is available in their annual reports and on their websites. In order to help researchers improve their chances of success, many of the councils also provide information on the criteria they use to assess awards. These are described further in Chapter 5. Before this, Chapter 4 looks at other major funders of research.

Table 3.1 Success rates for Research Council funding schemes, 2008–9 (2007–8 figures in brackets)

Research Council	Type of award	Success rate for awards made in 2008–09
AHRC	Standard research grants	12% (23%)
	Practice led & Applied research grants	33% (32%)
	Strategic initiatives large research grants (Religion & Society)	11% (9%)
	Strategic initiatives small research grants (Religion & Society)	24% (13%)
	Research Leave	20% (27%)
	Research Networks & workshops	30% (21%)
ESRC	Standard research grants	14% (15%)
	Small research grants	25% (36%)
	Fellowships	13% (26%)
EPSRC	Standard research grants	26% (32%)
	First grants scheme	31% (44%)
NERC	Standard & Small grants	23% (22%)
	Fellowships	19% (17%)
BBSRC	Project grants	16% (24%)
	Programme grants	44% (50%)
	New Investigator awards	20% (34%)
	Fellowships	10% (13%)
MRC	Research grants	20% (26%)
	New investigator awards	20% (24%)
	Senior non-clinical fellowships	12% (30%)
	Career Development Awards	15% (11%)

4

Who funds research?
Part 2: other funders

Medical research charities • Other charities and trusts • Professional associations • Government departments • Technology Strategy Board

The previous chapter focused on the UK Research Councils, as these are the primary funding organizations for many researchers within UK universities. Across all universities in the UK, around 25 per cent of their total research income (including QR) comes from the Research Councils. However, there are a number of other types of organization that also provide substantial funding for research, including charities, government departments, professional associations, industry and the European Union. In some cases (such as the Wellcome and Leverhulme Trusts), sponsoring research is the primary function of the organization, whereas in other cases (such as industry and commerce), sponsoring research helps the organizations to achieve their primary function. The current chapter provides an overview of some of these other funding organizations, and the forms of support they offer. Again, further information is available on the websites of the individual organizations (see Appendix 1 at page 159).

Although Research Council support is often seen as the 'gold standard' within universities, it is important for universities to have a diversity of funding sources. As an individual researcher you may also not want to become overly reliant on any one source. Another reason for considering non-Research Council funding sources is that many Research Councils will not allow you to resubmit revised unfunded applications, but these can be targeted at some of the organizations described below. For example, a strong application that does not quite make it for MRC or BBSRC support could, with some revision, be submitted to the Wellcome Trust. Furthermore, some of the organizations described below provide some forms of support, and fund research topics, that are not covered by the Research Councils.

Again, selection of an appropriate funding organization and scheme will depend on your personal motivation and the goals and nature of the proposed research. If you are at the start of your career, for example, you may require a small amount of funding to conduct a pilot study to put you in a position to apply for more substantial funding. The Nuffield and British Academy small grants schemes are appropriate in such cases. Early career researchers may also want funding so that you can purchase a particular piece of equipment to enable you to start to collect data; in which case the Royal Society scheme should be targeted. If you are a more advanced researcher, you might want help to collect pilot data to test out a new idea, and may benefit from support from either the Nuffield or Wellcome Trust undergraduate research bursary scheme. Support might also be wanted so that you can engage in new or existing research collaboration with researchers based overseas, in which case the Leverhulme Trust has a number of suitable schemes.

Medical research charities

A large number of medical charities sponsor research, some to a significant extent. Between around 2003 and 2008, medical charities spent over £3.25 billion on supporting research in the UK, contributing to our knowledge and understanding in the life sciences, medicine and health. Most medical research charities focus on specific illnesses and conditions, such as Alzheimer's disease, cancer and multiple sclerosis. Some are very small and only offer funding for very small projects, often in a rather ad hoc way, whereas others are large and have well developed systems for allocating research funding. Examples of these larger charities include the Alzheimer's Society, the Parkinson's Disease Society, the British Heart Foundation and Cancer Research UK. The British Heart Foundation, for example, spends over £100 million a year supporting a range of funding schemes, including project grants, programme grants, PhD studentships, fellowships, training awards and infrastructure grants.

The majority of the medical charities are members of the Association of Medical Research Charities (AMRC). The Association produces an annual handbook that provides useful information about the research schemes run by the different charities. Further information about potential funders can be found in this handbook and on the websites of the individual charities. By far the largest medical research charity is the Wellcome Trust, which sponsors research across a range of health conditions, and is therefore discussed in more detail here.

The Wellcome Trust

The Wellcome Trust was established in 1936, on the death of pharmaceutical entrepreneur Henry Wellcome, and is now the largest charity in the UK, with an endowment of around £15 billion. It funds innovative biomedical research, across all areas, in the UK and internationally, spending over £600 million each year. The largest single element of total funding is used to support basic curiosity driven, investigator led, research and career initiatives. It provides funding across the continuum of biomedical research to support basic and clinical research, and research in population health and medical humanities.

The Wellcome Trust supports both project and programme grants. Project grants provide funding for high quality, hypothesis driven projects in basic and clinical science, which are relevant to human and animal health. Awards are usually in the region of £150000 to £350000 over three years. Programme grants are again aimed at more experienced researchers with established track records, to provide an opportunity to concentrate on a larger programme of research. They provide support for five years for internationally competitive research relevant to human and animal health. The level of support awarded depends on the scientific needs of the proposed research, but awards do not normally exceed £1.2 million. You can apply for project or programme grants at any time during the year.

In addition, the Trust provides support for a large range of personal fellowships that are aimed at supporting researchers at different stages of career. If you are at an early stage of career, for example, you can apply for a Sir Henry Wellcome postdoctoral award. These are four-year awards, up to a maximum of £250 000. Support is provided for salary and some research expenses (see Chapter 6). If you are a little more advanced in your career and have between three and five years' postdoctoral research experience, you can apply for a Research Career Development Fellowship. These awards are held for five years and again provide support for salary and research expenses. Senior Research Fellowships in basic biomedical science or clinical science are also held for five years, and provide support for salary and a larger research programme. To be eligible, you should normally have between five and ten years' postdoctoral research experience. Finally, Principal Research Fellowships are the Trust's most prestigious awards, which are held by researchers of the highest international research standing. They provide support for seven years, and can be extended on a five-year rolling basis. In many instances the Trust will support individual researchers throughout their career development, for example by providing initial support through a Career Development Fellowship, followed by a Senior Research Fellowship and, in the case of the most successful researchers, a Principal Research Fellowship.

The Wellcome Trust also funds a number of other forms of research support, such as undergraduate research bursaries (which provide small amounts of funding to cover the costs of employing undergraduate students to work on a research project over the summer vacation period), public engagement activities, research symposia, conferences and workshops, biomedical resources (including databases and collections) and equipment. The latter includes capital funding for large-scale construction or refurbishment projects. The joint Wellcome Trust–Wolfson Foundation Capital Funding for Science Based Activities scheme, for example, provides capital funding for large-scale projects (above £1 million), in participation with the host institution.

Other charities and trusts

In addition to the medical research charities, a number of other charities and trusts support research. These include the Leverhulme Trust, the Nuffield Foundation and the Joseph Rowntree Foundation.

The Leverhulme Trust

The Leverhulme Trust was established following the death of Lord Leverhulme (a Victorian businessman and entrepreneur) in 1925. Originally, the Trust was part of Unilever PLC (formerly Lever Brothers), but since 1983 it has gained more independence. It now combines the direct initiatives of its trustees (who are drawn from the highest level within Unilever), made in the light of specialist peer review advice, together with a portfolio of awards made by a Research Awards Advisory Committee. The Trust covers all subject areas and offers a wide range of different types of support. With an annual income of around £40 million, it is among the largest all subject providers of research funding in the UK. When making awards and establishing assessment criteria, the trustees place special weight on the originality and significance of the proposed projects. They also favour work that attempts to remove barriers between traditional disciplines and therefore may be an appropriate source of funding for those of you working in new or emerging interdisciplinary areas.

The Trust's research project grants provide support for salaries of research staff and associated costs directly related to the project. The majority of awards involve a spend of up to £250K over a duration of two to three years. There is a two-stage application process, and outlines can be submitted at any time during the year. The Trust's research fellowships are open to experienced researchers, particularly those who are, or have been, prevented by routine duties from completing a programme of original research. Fellowships are tenable for between 3 and 24 months, and funding is provided up to a maximum of £45 000. The Trust also supports Major Research Fellowships in the Humanities and Social Sciences, Emeritus Fellowships (which allow senior established researchers who have retired to complete a project which began prior to their retirement) and Early Career Fellowships (which provide support for researchers who do not hold, and have not held, a permanent academic post). Finally, if you are looking for funding to support collaboration with partners overseas, the Trust provides funding for Visiting Fellowships and Professorships (which allow overseas scholars to spend time in the UK), Study Abroad Fellowships (which provide support for UK researchers to study abroad) and International Networks.

More detailed information about the Trust and the various schemes it supports can be found in its Guide to Funding.

The Nuffield Foundation

The Nuffield Foundation was established in 1943 by William Morris (Lord Nuffield), the founder of Morris Motors. The original aim of the Foundation was to advance social well-being, particularly through research and practical experiment, and it still aims to achieve this by supporting work which will bring about improvements in society, which is founded on careful reflection and informed by objective and reliable evidence. The Foundation's income (£9 million a year) comes from returns on its investments, and most of this is spent on grants for research or to support practical innovation and development, often in voluntary sector organizations. The Foundation looks for projects that are imaginative and innovative, take a thoughtful and rigorous approach to problems, and have potential to influence policy or practice. At the time of writing, for example, they are running programmes on access to justice and child protection and family justice.

The Foundation also runs a number of grant schemes that are targeted at specific purposes, such as providing support for early career social scientists through their small grants programme and New Career Development Fellowships. The latter support postdoctoral social scientists who have the potential to become outstanding in their field. Awards are made for research projects on issues of social significance, developed and carried out in partnership with an experienced social scientist. To be eligible, you must have no more than five years' postdoctoral research experience. The small grants scheme makes awards of, normally, up to a maximum of £7500, to support social science research experiments. The scheme favours projects that develop social science research capacity, and those that are self-contained pilot or preliminary projects that address the wider objectives of the Foundation.

One interesting scheme run by the Nuffield Foundation is its Science Bursaries for Undergraduate Research. The scheme allows students to gain first hand experience of carrying out research, under the supervision of a more experienced researcher. The advantage to the more experienced researcher (who has to apply for the award) is that you can gain some useful assistance, for example to test out pilot or preliminary ideas before submitting a larger scale proposal. Projects are normally carried out during the summer vacation preceding the student's final year of study, and funding is provided to help support the student's living costs while working on the project. As noted above, a similar scheme is run by the Wellcome Trust for academics whose research falls within the Trust's remit.

Joseph Rowntree Foundation

Finally, the Joseph Rowntree Foundation is one of the largest social policy research and development charities in the UK, and has supported research since 1959. Its aims are to examine the root causes of poverty and disadvantage and identify solutions, to find ways in which people and communities can have control of their lives, and to contribute to the building and development of strong cohesive and sustainable communities. The Foundation spends £10 million a year on its research and development programme. At any one time it supports a number of different research programmes in areas such as poverty, housing, independent living, long-term care of older people, alcohol and parenting. Applications are made in response to calls for proposals in targeted areas. Information about current programmes can be found on the Foundation's web pages.

Professional associations

Whereas the above Trusts and Foundations are independent of government, a small number of professional associations receive relatively small amounts of public funding to help them to pursue support for their disciplines. Two of the most well known of these are the Royal Society and the British Academy. Both provide funding for a limited number of research schemes.

The Royal Society

The Royal Society is the national academy of science of the UK and Commonwealth, and supports research across science, engineering and technology, and influences science policy. It was formally established in November 1660 and received its first government grant (£1000) in 1850 to assist scientists in their research and to buy equipment. The Society supports scientists from PhD level to senior professors, and offers grants for a variety of purposes from conference travel to the modernization of laboratories. If you are still relatively early in your research career, its research grant scheme provides awards of up to a maximum of £15000 to purchase equipment to support promising researchers. The Society also funds a number of Fellowships to enable talented young scientists to build their careers, and Research Professorships for more established researchers with outstanding track records. Both provide funding for salaries and research expenses. The Society also runs an International Grants

Programme to enable UK scientists to initiate collaborations with leading researchers overseas.

The British Academy

The British Academy, which was established in 1902, is the UK's national academy for the humanities and social sciences. Its funding strategy is focused on supporting ideas, individuals and intellectual resources, and it delivers this strategic priority through schemes for research grants, research posts, research development and conference grants. As an applicant, you must show that you are seeking support for advanced research at postdoctoral level and must normally be resident in the UK. Some of the academy's main funding schemes are as follows:

- *Small research grants* These provide a maximum of £7500 over two years to facilitate initial project planning and development, to support the direct costs of research, and to enable the enhancement of research through workshops, visits and the like.
- *Researcher Development Awards* These enable established scholars to develop a significant research project. Applications are particularly encouraged from scholars who can demonstrate that they are developing an innovative line of research with the potential to make a significant difference to their field and career profile. To be eligible to apply, you should normally have at least five years' postdoctoral research experience. The programme provides a flexible package of support for projects between £15000 and £150000, that last up to a maximum of three years.
- *Postdoctoral Fellowships* These enable outstanding early career researchers to strengthen their experience of research and teaching in a university environment. Awards cover salary and limited research expenses for a maximum of three years.
- *Joint Senior Research Fellowships with the Leverhulme Trust* These are one-year awards to allow established scholars a period of research leave to bring a major piece of research to completion. Support is provided for a full time replacement post to provide relief from university duties.

Government departments

Another significant source of research funding in the UK comes from Central Government departments. The departments provide funding to enable them to achieve their policy objectives, and the research they fund therefore tends to be strategic and applied in nature. Across its departments, the UK Government spends around £3.5 million on research and development each year, the largest proportion of which goes to the Ministry of Defence (MOD). Other large departments that support research include the Department of Health, which invests around £500 million per year in research and development, the Department for Environment, Food and Rural Affairs (DEFRA), the Department of Transport and the Home Office. Research funding is usually allocated on the basis of competitive tendering, following a public announcement or call. Such announcements usually set out the aims for the research and the timescale involved. It is often quite difficult to 'tap into' Government funding streams, as, despite the tendering process, many departments will support researchers with whom they have worked before or who have been recommended to them.

Some of the Research Councils support research that is carried out in collaboration with government departments, and this may be one way of getting easier access to Government department funding. Several, for example, provide support for joint Research Council/MOD research grants. These are intended to support research that is not only of high scientific quality but is also likely to be of relevance to the defence industries. The MOD provides up to 50 per cent of the costs of the research.

Until 2001, the MOD funded much university based research through its Defence Evaluation and Research Agency (DERA). In 2001, however, the Agency was divided into two separate parts – the Defence Science and Technology Laboratory (DSTL) and QinetiQ. DSTL is an agency of the MOD that exists to supply best impartial science and technical research and advice to the MOD and other Government departments. QinetiQ, in contrast, is now a commercial company that provides research, technical advice and technological solutions and services to customers in the core markets of defence and security. Much of its work is done in partnership with university researchers and departments.

The National Health Service

Research within the NHS is now coordinated by the National Institute of Health Research (NIHR), which was established in 2006. The NIHR operates a Central Commissioning Facility (NIHR-CCF), which is a primary gateway for health researchers seeking funding from the NHS. There is an emphasis within the NIHR that the research it supports encompasses patient and public involvement in some way. The NIHR runs a number of specific research programmes and also manages the NIHR-supported research centres and services. Research programmes include the following:

- *Programme Grants for Applied Research* These are prestigious, substantial open awards for leading research groups able to demonstrate a strong track record of achievement in applied health research to tackle high priority health issues. Awards are for a maximum of £2 million over a period of up to five years. The NIHR also offers smaller Programme Development Grants (ranging from £20 000 to £100 000) to provide support to enable a research team to undertake preparatory work that will position them better to submit a successful Programme Grant application.

- *Invention for Innovation awards* This programme is a direct response to the need to accelerate the innovation process. The programme combines the former New and Emerging Applications of Technology (NEAT) and Health Technology Devices (HTD) programmes. The Invention for Innovation programme funds translational research, extending between basic research and pre-clinical trials or health technology assessments. There are three funding streams, running from up to £100 000 to support feasibility studies or commercial viability studies, through £150 000 to £250 000 for applied research projects, to up to £3000 000 for collaborative applied research projects.
- *Research for Patient Benefit (RfPB) programme* This is a nationally coordinated funding stream for regionally commissioned NHS research. RfPB projects investigate ways to improve patients' experience of the NHS through research in the following areas:
  ° the way that NHS services are provided and used;
  ° the effectiveness and value of interventions;
  ° alternative means for providing healthcare;
  ° innovations and developments in health and social care.

There are ten regional funding committees, with budgets that vary according to the size of the regional population. Each research project can run up to a maximum of three years with funding for up to £250 000. Many university based researchers are involved in RfPB projects, but the projects must always be led by an NHS partner and all funding goes via the NHS Trust or Trusts involved.

- *Research for Innovation, Speculation and Creativity (RISC)* This programme supports new and radical research proposals with the potential to create a step change in the way patients are cared for, managed and treated. It awards grants for speculative, novel projects that have the potential for high impact but which are unlikely to gain support during traditional peer review processes. In this way, the programme complements the Research for Patient Benefit programme by providing a stream for applications that are, as yet, too speculative for RfPB support.

All NHS funding schemes require collaboration with NHS researchers and healthcare Trusts, and the vast majority require the research project to be led by, and based in, the NHS Trust. Without good contacts in such organizations it is very difficult if you are an academic researcher to gain NHS funding for research.

The European Union

The UK's most significant source of overseas support for university based research comes from the EU. The majority of university based research supported through the EU is funded via its Framework Programme, now in its seventh phase (Framework Programme 7 – FP7). Research funded under the programme must have relevance to European policies such as European harmonization, economic competitiveness, European enlargement, social and cultural aspects concerning the quality of life, environment, employment, health and technology. There must also be added value for Europe in the proposed research collaboration, and projects need to demonstrate that it is only possible to achieve the goals of the research with EU support. The Seventh Framework programme is the EU's main instrument for funding research in Europe and runs from 2007 to 2013. It has a total budget of 50 billion Euros, which represents a 60 per cent increase in EU funding over the previous FP6.

The majority of FP7 funding is being used to support transnational collaborative research projects (through its Co-operation Programme) in ten broad science areas (health; food, agriculture and fisheries biotechnology; information and communication technologies; nanoscience and nanotechnology; energy; environment; transport; socio-economic sciences and humanities; space; and security). Each theme is operationally autonomous, and each has been selected to reflect the most important fields in knowledge and technology where research excellence is particularly important to improve Europe's ability to address its social, economic, public health, environment and industrial challenges of the future. Projects are carried out by consortia which include participants from several different EU (and other) countries. Awards are made on the basis of open calls for proposals and a peer review process.

In addition to this Co-operation Programme, FP7 also supports an Ideas Programme, a People Programme and a Capacities Programme:

- The Ideas Programme supports 'frontier research' solely on the basis of scientific excellence. Research may be carried out in any area of science, technology, socio-economic sciences and humanities. There is no obligation under this programme for cross-border partnerships. The Ideas Programme is implemented via the new European Research Council (see below).
- The People Programme provides support for research mobility and career development. It is implemented via a set of Marie Curie actions, providing fellowships and other measures to help researchers to build their skills and competences. The programme includes support for Marie Curie Networks, Industry-Academe partnerships, Intra-European Fellowships, Outgoing and Incoming Fellowships, and the International Cooperation Scheme.
- The Capacities Programme is aimed at strengthening the research capacities that Europe needs to be a thriving knowledge based economy, including funding for research infrastructure and research that benefits small and medium size enterprises (SMEs).

Information about calls for proposals for all of the different programmes can be found in the EU's official journal. A useful source of information for UK based researchers is the Community Research and Development Information Service (CORDIS). Further information is available from the UK Research Office (UKRO); your institution may well subscribe to this organization.

Applying for FP7 support is a complex process, particularly in the case of large collaborative projects. Successful applicants are more likely to be those working in well established collaborative teams, led by a strong experienced coordinator with a high level of administrative support. Although there is a facility for individual researchers to find potential project partners via the CORDIS website, you should be wary of embarking on the process of trying to gain FP7 support for your research if you are new to the Framework Programme and do not have good collaborative links. An advantage of engaging in EU FP7 projects is that they usually involve relatively large amounts of research income. However, even for experienced researchers, there are also a number of disadvantages that researchers and institutions need to take into account. In addition to the large amount of bureaucracy involved in applying for and managing projects, FP7 funding does not cover the full economic costs of the research, nor does it provide funding to cover the costs of any sick pay losses that might be incurred during the course of a project. Furthermore, their schemes that provide support for postgraduate research studentships do not allow institutions to claim for the fees element of awards.

The European Research Council

The European Research Council (ERC) began to take shape in 2003 and was officially launched in February 2007. It issued its first call for proposals in April of that year, and received nearly 10000 applications from researchers across Europe. The Council supports investigator driven, frontier research in all areas. Its main aim is to stimulate scientific excellence by supporting and encouraging the very best scientists, scholars and engineers to take risks in research and go beyond established frontiers of knowledge and boundaries of their disciplines. It allows researchers to identify opportunities and new directions in any field of research. Grants are awarded through open competition to researchers working in, or moving to, Europe. The ERC offers two main types of grant – Starting Independent Researcher grants and Advanced Investigator grants.

Starting Independent Researcher grants support up and coming research leaders who are about to establish, or consolidate, a proper research team and start to conduct independent research in Europe. The grants are targeted at highly promising researchers who have the proven potential of becoming independent research leaders in any field of science, engineering and scholarship. To be eligible as principal investigator, you must have obtained a PhD between three and eight years of the date of the call. Grants are made up to a maximum of 2 million Euros and run for up to five years. There is an annual call for proposals in summer each year.

Advanced Investigator grants, in contrast, are targeted at researchers who have already established themselves as independent research leaders in their own right, and who want to carry out frontier research on a topic of their choice. Awards are made up to a maximum of 3.5 million Euros and again run for up to five years. There is an annual call for proposals in autumn each year. Both Starting Independent Researcher grants and Advanced Investigator grants are exceedingly competitive schemes with relatively low success rates, and so you should only consider applying if you have a very strong track record for your stage of career.

The NATO Science Programme

An international scheme that goes beyond Europe is the NATO Science Programme, which supports scientists of the countries of the Euro-Atlantic Partnership Council (EAPC) in cooperative science and research infrastructure development. Its purpose is to stimulate the cooperation essential to progress in science, to protect the human resources of the science community in partner countries and to contribute to overall peace and security. Support under the science programme is through collaborative activities designed to create enduring links between researchers in partner and NATO countries. Applications are considered by advisory panels of experts from different NATO and partner countries. Further information is available on the Programme's website.

Industry and business

Industry and business fund a far greater proportion of UK research than does UK Government, and also carry out the greatest proportion of research in the UK, more than three times the amount carried out by HEIs. Most industries invest in research as it is important for them to keep developing new products and processes to support their business. Some industrial sectors, such as pharmaceutical, information technology and aerospace, have a long history of doing this, whereas others have less experience of either carrying out their own research or working in partnership with universities.

Businesses rarely support blue skies research. Most of their support is for applied research, carried out under research contracts. As we saw in Chapter 2, such research is contracted under a specific well-defined set of conditions and requirements, against a fixed timescale, with measured outputs. The purpose of the contract is to agree before a project begins on a framework for reaching a common understanding of each party's commitments and responsibilities. Contracts are legally binding and usually cover matters such as price, perform-ance, liability, ownership of intellectual property, project management and timescale. Businesses rarely call for applications for their funding. Rather, pro-jects either arise out of existing relationships between academic and business partners or stem from new partnerships that are formed to help address the needs of the business. In most cases, the specific nature of the project and proposed workplan will result from a series of interactions between the two parties, rather than being fully specified by one side or the other (see Chapter 10). The majority of UK universities now have Business Development offices or the equivalent that are set up to help academics to establish and maintain links with appropriate business partners. If you have a potential project that you feel would be of interest to an industry or business it is important to discuss your ideas with someone from your Business Development office. Trying to 'go it alone' and cold calling round different businesses can be a long and fruitless process.

Government support for promoting business–knowledge base collaborations

Like many governments in the developed world, UK Government provides a number of support mechanisms for promoting links between businesses and universities and other research based organizations. LINK awards, for example, are a national scheme to promote industry–academic collaboration in pre-competitive research. Their aim is to accelerate the commercial exploitation of government funded pre-competitive research and to focus on advances in science and engineering with particular commercial promise. Projects are typically funded 50 per cent by the industry concerned and 50 per cent by Government. A number of Research Councils participate in the scheme. BBSRC, for example, contributes around £3 million a year to funding LINK awards. Advantages for the industry include financial support towards the costs of projects, closer relationships with the science base and the possibility of recruiting trained personnel at the end of the project. Advantages for you as the academic partner would include access to industry based expertise and facilities, and an opportunity to forge larger, longer term, partnerships with the organizations concerned, in addition to financial support for the research itself.

Several of the Research Councils also run a number of other schemes for promoting university–business links, ranging from support for individual responsive mode applications to support for larger strategic partnerships between businesses and academic partners. BBSRC, for example, runs an Industrial Partnership Award (IPA) scheme. IPAs are science-led, responsive mode grants that address scientific questions within any area of its remit. To be eligible, the industrial partner must contribute, in cash, at least 10 per cent of the full economic cost of the project. To be successful as an applicant, you have to demonstrate the value of the academic–industry partnership that underpins the proposed project, including details of the scientific benefits to each side. Applications are assessed by the relevant Research Council committee alongside standard responsive mode applications, using the same criteria, but may receive a strategic uplift against standard grants of an equivalent scientific merit. If you are working in an appropriate area, you can therefore increase your chance of success if you can secure a relatively modest level of industrial investment in your research.

MRC has similarly recently launched a new approach to funding col-laborative research between academia and industry – the MRC Industry Collaborative Award (MICA). MICA applications can be submitted to any of the Council's funding schemes (e.g. programme grants, research grants, Development Pathway awards) for which the lead applicant (who must be the academic partner) is eligible. Funding decisions are made on the basis of scien-tific quality, whether the funding required and collaboration are essential for the planned research to go ahead, and demonstration of good management of potential conflicts of interest and appropriate distribution of Intellectual Property (IP). Proposals fall into two categories:

- *Fully Flexible* This is where there is no minimum level of industrial partner's contribution, and IP is fully allocated to the academic partner.
- *Gated Contributions* This is where the value of the industrial contribution must be above a certain level (either 25 or 50 per cent, depending on type of project) and where the industrial partner pre-negotiates the distribu-tion of IP.

Several of the councils also provide funding to support academic–industry collaborations through various fellowship and exchange schemes. BBSRC, for example, operates an Enterprise Fellowship Scheme that may be applicable if you are keen to commercialize your research. Similarly, ESRC supports a Business Placement Fellowship scheme, which provides funding so that you could spend time in a business organization to undertake practice-relevant research and work with the business sector on a specific project. The durations of fellowships range from one to twelve months. ESRC also supports a Social Science Workplace Experience programme, which offers undergraduate and postgraduate social science students the opportunity to undertake eight-week placements during the summer months in SMEs, local authorities and third sector organizations. Placement projects focus on supporting organizations with their research, strategy or business development requirements, and pro-vide an opportunity for students to develop their skills outside the normal academic environment.

CASE studentships

Another form of encouraging and supporting academic–business collabo-ration is the CASE (Collaborative Awards in Science and Engineering) stu-dentship scheme, which is operated by most of the UK Research Councils. Although the awards were originally aimed at the science and engineering disciplines, they now extend much more broadly, covering social science as well. The different councils run the scheme in different ways. ESRC, for example, runs an annual competition for CASE studentships to support postgraduate research projects in the social sciences. Applicants have to be based in CASE-recognized academic departments. Non-academic partners can be private sector, public or voluntary bodies. The academic and non-academic partners submit a joint application that outlines a specific project that will be carried out during the course of the studentship. The partners also have to detail the research training that will be provided, as well as supervisory arrangements, and other support. The majority of the funding for the studentship is provided by the Research Council, with the non-academic partner making an annual contribution which has to be above a set minimum amount (around £4000). Some of the Research Councils also run Industrial CASE studentships, where the lead partner has to be the industrial partner rather than the academic. Whatever the particular form of award, CASE studentships are useful for establishing and building relationships between academic and non-academic partners, and for piloting relatively small-scale research projects at a reasonably low cost for the non-academic partner. In addition, they are increasingly becoming one of the limited number of schemes that allow individual academics to apply for funding to support a research studentship.

Technology Strategy Board

Finally in this section, the UK's Technology Strategy Board (TSB) is responsible for promoting, coordinating and supporting business–academic collaborations. The TSB is an executive non-departmental public body, whose role is to stimulate technology-enabled innovation in areas which offer the greatest scope for boosting UK growth and productivity. The activities of the TSB are jointly funded by the Department for Innovation, Universities and Skills (DIUS) and other Government Departments, Regional Development Agencies, and the Research Councils. It invests in projects involving businesses and research working together to deliver successful technology based products and services. In order to focus its support in priority areas, it has identified a number of Key Application Areas (such as environmental sustainability, energy generation and supply, medicines and healthcare, creative industries, transport, and built environment) and Key Technology Areas (such as high value manufacturing, advanced materials, nanotechnology, bioscience, electronics photonics and electrical systems, and information and communication technology).

Two of its major programmes are Knowledge Transfer Networks and Knowledge Transfer Partnerships. A Knowledge Transfer Network (KTN) is a single overarching national network in a specific field of technology or business application which brings together people from businesses, universities, research, finance and technology organizations to stimulate innovation through knowledge transfer. There are currently 23 KTNs running, with a total membership of around 30000. The objective of a KTN is to improve the UK's innovation performance by increasing the breadth and depth of knowledge transfer of technology into UK based businesses by accelerating the rate at which the process occurs. The Network must, throughout its lifetime, actively contribute and remain aligned to the goals of the TSB.

The Knowledge Transfer Partnership (KTP) scheme, formerly known as the Teaching Company Scheme, provides major support for partnerships between (usually individual) industries and universities, in which technology is transferred and embodied in a particular company by the use of trained personnel. Projects can be undertaken in a wide range of areas, including product and service design, manufacturing, technology innovation, business processes (including information technology and social science) and commercial development. Businesses of all sizes and in most industrial and commercial sectors can take part. A KTP typically involves forming a partnership between a company and an academic institution, enabling the company to access the skills and expertise held by the academic institution. Individual projects normally last between one and three years and are partially funded by a government grant, via the TSB. The company also has to contribute a proportion of the funding, with the amount depending on its size. SMEs, for example, would typically be expected to contribute around one-third of the costs (with an average contribution of around £20K). Larger companies may contribute up to half. The largest part of the funding is spent on supporting the salary of one or more KTP associate (i.e. a trained graduate who works on a specific project within the company under the supervision of the academic partner as well as the company). Most universities now have dedicated staff who can help you to access potential partners and apply for such awards.

Chapter 10 returns to the subject of academic–business collaborations, and also considers the commercial exploitation of research.

5

Assessment of proposals – what will happen to your application?

Assessment of proposals by the UK Research Councils • Other research funders • The submission and review process • Is peer review effective? • The validity of peer review

In order to be able to prepare a competitive application, you need to understand the process of what happens to your application once it has been submitted and, particularly, the criteria that will be used to assess it. Hence, the current chapter outlines the main processes and criteria that are used, before we move on to considering how to prepare a competitive application. The majority of applications that you submit will undergo some form of peer review; that is, they will be subject to assessment by fellow academics with specialist knowledge of the area of the proposed research. In most cases, assessors will be asked to judge the potential of the research outlined in the application, rather than simply evaluating previous research outcomes. All of the UK Research Councils and major trusts and charities make extensive use of the peer review process. Most have set up specialist boards, panels and/or colleges of experts to help them ensure that peer review is carried out in an appropriate, informed and unbiased way. Although different funding organizations use slightly different methods and criteria when assessing the merit of proposals, the majority adhere to a number of common principles, such as making assessment criteria transparent, treating proposals in confidence, selecting reviewers who have expert knowledge of the subject area and, in most cases, allowing applicants the right to reply to reviewers' comments before funding decisions are made. Similarly, most proposals will be assessed in terms of their scientific excellence and importance of the proposed research, its fit with the mission and priorities of the funding body, the timeliness and promise of the project, its cost effectiveness and, increasingly, its potential economic and social impact.

Assessment of proposals by the UK Research Councils

Each of the Research Councils gives detailed information about their peer review process on their web pages, and applicants should thoroughly familiarize themselves with this material. The information includes details of the nature and membership of any grants panels and wider peer review colleges, as well as information about the use of expert referees to review their grant submissions. Many of the councils also provide a useful questions and answers section for applicants. As will be made clear in Chapter 7, as an applicant, you need to know the specific criteria according to which your proposal will be assessed, before starting to prepare your application, if you are to stand any chance of success. Chapter 7 also provides advice on how to respond convincingly to referees' comments, if you are given the opportunity to do this.

Grants panels

All of the Research Councils use some form of grants panels to help them assess proposals. In most cases they run standing panels, with members who serve for a fixed period of time (usually three or four years). The panels are often based on broad disciplinary groupings. MRC, for example, has four grants boards: infections and immunity, molecular and cellular medicine, neurosciences and mental health, and population systems and medicine. Similarly, BBSRC has recently restructured its grants committees into five groups: animal systems; health and well-being; plants, microbes, food and sustainability; technological and methodological developments; and molecules, cells and industrial biotechnology. ESRC, in contrast, has one overall Research Grants Board which covers the breadth of their responsive mode activity across the entire social sciences. Other councils, such as EPSRC, do not have standing grants panels but constitute panels from the membership of their expert college to deal with applications in a particular round. The above panels and boards primarily handle responsive mode applications. Many of the councils will also have other boards and committees to help them shape and assess directed mode research (e.g. targeted research programmes) as well as handle other funding competitions (e.g. fellowships). Other major funding organizations also have standing grants panels and committees. The Wellcome Trust, for example, has six grants committees: immunology and infectious diseases; populations and public health; cognitive and higher systems; molecular and cellular neurosciences; physiological sciences; and molecules, genes and cells.

In most cases, peer review grants panels judge the relative quality of research proposals based on their own background knowledge and, usually, assessments from peer reviewers with expertise in the area of the proposal. The panels are normally responsible for placing the proposals that are competing for funding in the funding round or competition in a priority order. Decisions will then be made on the basis of this priority listing and the amount of funding available for allocation. To keep workload manageable, some Research Councils use preliminary triage type procedures which screen out some of the applications, on the basis of referees' scores and comments, so that only the higher scoring ones are considered by the assessment panel. With targeted research programmes (often where large numbers of applications are expected), the councils frequently employ the use of outline proposals, with committee members making preliminary short-listing decisions on the basis of the outlines (without the benefit of referees' reports). Short-listed applicants are then invited to submit full proposals, which are sent out for expert review, before committee members make final funding recommendations. Grants boards and committees typically allocate a number of proposals to each panel member, who will be required to lead discussion, summarizing the views of the referees and any response to reviewers' comments that is provided by the applicant. They will typically comment on any major discrepancies between different reviewers, pointing out if they feel that particular reviewers' comments are not of sufficient quality to help inform decision making, and if they feel the reviewer in question is not an appropriate person to be assessing the application. Lead members may also be asked to provide an indicative rating score or grade. Other panel members will then contribute to discussion before the panel agrees a final score or grading.

Panel members also typically play a role in the assessment of end of grant reports (and mid-term reports in the case of longer programme grants), where they are asked to judge whether the applicant has delivered on set objectives, as well as to assess the quality of the research that has been carried out (including any research outputs). Some of the Research Councils consider these assessments when making decisions about subsequent proposals from the applicant.

Given the diversity of areas covered by any one panel, any one member will have to comment on proposals across a broad range of areas. You need to bear this in mind when framing and presenting your proposal (see Chapter 7). Finally, as a potential applicant, you may well hear rumours about how particular grants panels work and particular biases they may have.

In my experience, most such rumours are unfounded and it is generally better to ignore them.

Peer review colleges

A number of the Research Councils have established peer review colleges to aid them in the overall assessment process. Membership is determined on the basis of nominations from institutions, user bodies and the scientific community. Most members serve for limited terms of office (three or four years) and there is replacement of a certain proportion of members each year. Most members receive some form of training in addition to detailed written guidance. Some of the Research Councils select referees and potential grants panel members from their college. EPSRC for example has an established college of around 4000 researchers and users of research, who normally remain on the college for four years. NERC's college is smaller, with around 370 members, and is used to provide assessments, advice and guidance across the full spectrum of NERC's research. In addition to being involved in the assessment of specific proposals, and sitting on particular committees, established members may also become involved in advising on policy issues. MRC College of Experts is made up of more than 1000 expert scientists, who have agreed to review a minimum of six research proposals each year. The college also provides a pool of expertise for MRC reviews of specific research topics or five-yearly reviews of MRC units, or evaluation of the impact of MRC-funded research. Some members are also appointed to Research Training and Development interview panels.

Reviewers

All of the Research Councils use expert reviewers to assist their grants boards and committees to make funding recommendations. Some draw their reviewers primarily from their peer review colleges, but may extend this by using additional (sometimes overseas based) subject experts. Reviewers are selected because they have expertise in the subject area of the proposal under consideration, and often because they have experience of gaining research income from the funding organization. Typically, between three and six individuals will be asked to comment on any one proposal. In some cases, referees who are users of research might be selected, in addition to those with academic expertise. Most of the councils allow applicants to suggest the names of potential referees, and they typically use one or two of these in addition to the referees that they have identified. When selecting potential referees, funding bodies need to avoid known conflicts of interest (such as asking reviewers to assess proposals from applicants based in their own institution, or from known collaborators). In addition, referees are asked to declare any further potential conflicts of interest when submitting their comments. Reviewers' identities are not revealed to applicants, and often not to panel members until after initial grading has taken place. Reviewers are generally provided with detailed guidance information (which is often available on the council's web pages), including the criteria by which they should assess proposals, the rating scale to be used, the form in which they should format their responses, and information about codes of conduct, such as treating proposals 'in confidence'. BBSRC's website also includes an example of a completed review report. This is a useful source of information, not only for referees, but also for applicants.

Gaining experience as a reviewer, or being a member of a peer review college or grants committee, is a very useful way for you to learn about the grant getting process, and to find out about the way of thinking of the funding organization. You will see examples of strong, well written and persuasively argued proposals, as well as examples of poorly argued and presented cases. From these, you can start to distil what makes a good proposal and what makes a poor one.

Standard peer review criteria

Most of the Research Councils use similar criteria when assessing proposals, particularly in their responsive mode competitions. In general these cover the scientific excellence or overall quality of the proposed research (including its novelty and timeliness), the fit to the remit and priorities of the funding organization, the soundness of the methodology, the track record of the applicant and host institution and the cost effectiveness of the project. Some illustrative examples of criteria used in relation to assessing responsive mode applications for four of the Research Councils are shown in Appendixes 4 to 7. Further information for these councils, and also those not covered here, is available on their websites.

It is important for you to ensure that you prepare proposals with the specific criteria that will be used by the relevant funder in mind. If novelty and timeliness are key criteria, then spell out what the novel aspects are and why it is particularly important that the research is conducted at this time. If the council is interested in the project's potential for staff training, then make it clear what any research staff will learn and what skills they will acquire while working on the project. Similarly, if reviewers are being asked to comment on your track record and ability to carry out and manage the project, make sure that your relevant previous experience is highlighted.

Additional criteria used in other competitions

Many of the criteria shown in Appendixes 4 to 7 will also be used in relation to other funding competitions run by the councils. In addition, the councils will often employ further criteria that relate specifically to the nature of the funding scheme in question or the type of support being requested. In the case of bids that are aimed at directed research programmes, for example, the

Research Councils are likely to employ the same, or very similar, criteria to assess scientific excellence, as they would for responsive mode applications, but they will also ask assessors to comment on how well the proposed research would contribute to meeting the specific aims and objectives of the programme in question. This will include not only the scientific aims and objectives, but also broader aims (where relevant) such as encouraging multidisciplinary approaches to address the aims, or training the next generation of researchers, or meeting other capacity building aims.

In the case of applications for larger programmes of activity (such as EPSRC's platform grants, or BBSRC's Larger, Longer Awards), additional criteria will be applied to assess issues such as the extent to which the applicants/research team are international leaders in their field, with a strong record of grant support, and are led by the right person; the scope for developing and promoting the careers of research staff who will be associated with the programme; and the proposed management arrangements. They will also take account of the level of co-funding and other types of support offered by the host institution and other organizations, and the extent to which the Research Council funding (in the form of one large grant) would result in significant added value. There is no point even considering applying to one of these schemes unless your track record and standing is appropriate.

Finally, a number of Research Council funding schemes are more person- than project-based. This includes the wide range of fellowships that the councils support (see Chapter 3). Many of the criteria for these will focus on assessing the suitability of the person, him- or herself, and the surrounding research environment, in addition to the strength of the proposed project. Box 5.1 shows the additional criteria used by the MRC to assess the person and institution components of applications.

Box 5.1 Criteria used by MRC to assess person and institution components of research fellowship applications

- Has the applicant demonstrated their independence as a research scientist?
- Has the applicant demonstrated their potential as a high calibre researcher?
- Does the applicant have the ability to carry out the proposed work?
- Has the applicant shown that they can effectively lead a research team?
- (and for senior fellowships) Does the applicant show significant potential of becoming a leader in their field of research?
- What is the standing of the proposed Centre in the field of research in question?
- Is the Centre an appropriate one for the proposed project and career goals of the applicant?
- (where relevant) What is the quality of the training that the applicant would be likely to receive there?

Similarly, in the case of BBSRC's Research Development and Professorial Fellowship schemes, in addition to assessing proposed projects, referees are asked to comment on aspects such as the applicant's research and personal achievements to date (e.g. the number and quality of publications, collaborations with other scientists in academia and industry, and prizes, honours and grants held). They are also asked to comment on the added value of awarding a fellowship. Interestingly, referees/assessors for ESRC's Professorial Fellowships are asked to form judgements primarily on the basis of the Fellow's ability to produce exciting and ground-breaking research outcomes. Assessments regarding creativity and innovation are of paramount importance, rather than focusing primarily on the specific research questions and proposed methodology.

The assessment of impact

Traditionally, the success (or otherwise) of academic research has been judged in a relatively narrow way; primarily in terms of its contribution to the academic knowledge base. However, since around 2007 questions are increasingly being asked about the wider impact and benefits of research, such as 'what is the economic, social or cultural impact?', 'how does the research contribute to policy or practice?'. The Research Councils define 'economic impact' broadly as:

> the demonstrable contribution that excellent research makes to society and the economy. This accords with the Royal Charters of the Councils and with HM Treasury guidance on the appraisal of economic impact. Impact embraces all the extremely diverse ways in which research-related knowledge and skills benefit individuals, organisations, and nations by fostering global economic performance, and specifically the economic competitiveness of the UK; increasing the effectiveness of public services and policy; and enhancing quality of life, health and creative output
> (see, e.g. EPSRC 2009).

In line with this emphasis, the UK Research Councils have recently amended their research grant application forms and peer review process to assess wider impact.

Early in 2009, for example, ESRC announced that it expects the researchers it funds to identify the potential scientific, societal and economic impact of their research, and to actively consider how these can be maximized and developed, and the council has modified its assessment process to reflect this. At the same time, however, it pointed out that 'excellent research without obvious or immediate societal or economic impact will not be disadvantaged in the assessment process' and that 'the principal criterion for funding decisions will remain the scientific quality of the proposed research' (ESRC 2009). If you apply for an ESRC project grant, you are now asked to produce an 'impact summary' (who will benefit from the research and how), and an 'impact planning statement' (what will you do to ensure benefit), in addition to the standard academic summary statement. The impact summary and plan allow you to highlight potential pathways to impact and allow the Research Councils to support you in these activities. The councils are not expecting you to predict the specific future benefits of your research. The emphasis is on ensuring that, where there is potential for wider impact, there are mechanisms and plans in place for this impact to be realized. In line with this, peer reviewers are now being invited to comment on whether the plans to maximize potential impacts are appropriate and justified, given the nature of the proposed research.

Similarly, if you apply to AHRC you will now be asked to describe who will benefit from the research, how they will benefit, and what you will do to ensure the benefit. AHRC provides examples of the sorts of impacts that might be expected from arts and humanities researchers. These include collaborations with organizations such as museums, libraries and heritage centres, creative and performing arts companies, commercial companies, charities and voluntary organizations, hospitals and healthcare organizations, schools and colleges, tourism and heritage organizations, faith groups, media organizations and prisons. In order to assess potential impact, reviewers and assessors are asked to consider both the excellence and impact characteristics of applications when commenting on, and prioritizing, proposals for funding, in competition with other proposals.

You should not be put off by having to think about the potential impact of your research. After all, most researchers do want their research to have impact and to be of value to others. The key thing is to remember that if your research does have potential impact, either for the economy, society, culture or whatever, it is important to show that you have thought about what you will do to ensure that it is realized. If the potential non-academic impact is not immediately obvious, then be open about this. Remember, it is not expected that every single fundable application will have immediate non-academic impact.

Other research funders

The preceding sections have focused on the Research Councils, as they are major funders of research in the UK, and because information on their assessment criteria is readily available. It can be seen from the descriptions of the various criteria that the councils use broadly similar criteria when assessing proposals. It is probably not surprising that similar criteria are also used by other major funding organizations when assessing applications. The Wellcome Trust (the largest medical research charity), for example, asks referees to address the following when assessing responsive mode applications:

- the importance of the research question, considering its originality and potential impact;
- the feasibility of the methods proposed to address the research question, considering whether the research is deliverable;
- the standing of the applicant and his or her potential to deliver the proposed research.

Reviewers are asked to give a grading (outstanding, excellent, competitive, satisfactory, supportable, not supportable) to each of the above aspects. They are also asked whether the request for resources is appropriate and justified. In the case of equipment, resource and technology development grants, referees are also asked to comment on the need for/added value of the equipment, the applicants' suitability to undertake or manage the resource, the appropriateness of the proposed technical support and access arrangements and the long term sustainability of the equipment.

The British Academy provides detailed information about its assessment criteria, for all of its funding schemes, on its website. Applications for its popular small grants scheme, for example, are assessed primarily on the basis of the originality and scholarly importance of the proposed research, the relationship to (and volume of) existing research in the field, the suitability of the methodology and feasibility of the programme, and intended outcomes. Assessors also take account of the track record of the applicant (primarily in terms of publications) and their stage of career. Criteria for its fellowship schemes are based on assessing the distinction, or potential distinction, of the candidate and the quality of the proposed research project. In the case of postdoctoral fellowships, assessors are asked to consider whether the candidate has the potential to go on after the award to a successful academic career and whether they are proposing to work in a suitable host institution.

Some smaller funding organizations may have criteria that are more specifically linked to their particular charitable or corporate objectives. To be successful with these organizations, you need to ensure that you are aware of these when writing your proposal. The key message is that, irrespective of funder, you will only produce a competitive proposal if you write it in the light of knowing the criteria by which it will be judged.

The submission and review process

With the exception of the MRC, which uses its own electronic application system, the Research Councils use a common electronic system (the Joint Electronic Submission, Je-S, system) to handle grant submissions. Access to this system is provided through university administrative offices (usually research support offices), and applications have to be 'signed off' by a designated 'officer' who has authority to do this. Similarly, the Wellcome Trust uses an electronic E-Grants submission system. More details on these systems will be provided in Chapter 7. The chapter also provides information on what happens to applications once they have been received by the funding organization. The time taken from submission to funding decisions will vary depending on the particular funding organization in question and the funding competition. In most cases, however, decisions take around six months. As noted in Chapter 4, some of the Research Councils have open date responsive mode competitions, where applications can be submitted at any time. However, the timing of grants panels is usually fixed well in advance and so office staff will be able to advise on 'unofficial deadlines' by which proposals will need to be submitted in order to be considered in a specific round. Other councils have fixed date schemes, sometimes run in two stages (outline and full proposal). With some of the larger programmes and research investments, the councils may include a final interview stage, in which short-listed applicants will be required to answer questions about their proposal. Further information about preparing for such interviews is provided in Chapter 7.

Is peer review effective?

Implementing and running an appropriate and effective peer review system can be a major undertaking for funding organizations. EPSRC, for example, receives and processes around 5500 applications a year. In recent years, there has therefore been growing concern about the burden and effectiveness of the peer review process. A report by the Royal Society, published in 2005, concluded that peer review remained the most effective mechanism for taking funding decisions, but also acknowledged the burden it places on the community, particularly when success rates are low. In 2006, RCUK decided to commission its own study to analyse the full economic cost of the Research Council peer review process and the potential for improving its efficiency while maintaining its effectiveness. The study covered all of the Research Councils and took account of all aspects of the review process, including the assessment of final reports. The results showed a total cost to the UK of preparing and reviewing proposals and reports for Research Council funding of £196 million per year (around 6 per cent of the total money distributed by the councils). The vast majority of the load fell on universities, primarily in terms of preparing and submitting proposals. Less than £10 million of the total costs were incurred by the Research Councils themselves. Despite the time involved in preparing proposals and reviewing those of others, the vast majority of researchers sampled felt that peer review was a good system and that preparing proposals was a worthwhile activity.

The study concluded that the results provide strong endorsement of the effectiveness of peer review in allocating funding wisely and fairly. However, while validating the continued use of peer review, it also noted the potential for further improvements with respect to referee selection, the speed of decision making, support of high risk research and giving feedback to applicants. The study also considered a number of options to improve the efficiency of the process, primarily in terms of reducing the number of applications or the time involved in reviewing. The four options that were thought to be worth further consideration were:

- introducing more consolidation so that the councils would award fewer larger, longer grants;
- introducing institutional level quotas on number of applications that could be submitted in any one year;
- reducing the number of resubmitted proposals (i.e. that were not funded on first submission);
- increasing the use of outline proposals.

Given the potentially controversial nature of some of the proposals, RCUK decided to consult with the community on the four options. The results of the consultation showed overwhelming support for peer review, with respondents believing that the quality of UK peer review was very high. As far as the proposed options were concerned, only a relatively small number of respondents were in favour of introducing further consolidation, and virtually all were against the idea of introducing institutional level quotas. There was, however, significant support for the proposal to reduce the number of resubmissions by restricting these to invited resubmissions only. There was also support for the greater use of outline proposals.

RCUK published a response to the consultation in June 2007 (RCUK 2007b). In terms of the four options, they stated that they may introduce a further degree of consolidation in areas where it is appropriate for the research and funding mechanism, and that they would increase the use of outlines in managed funding modes (rather than in responsive mode). They also agreed to do more to share good practice, publicize success rates and reduce the overall burden of the final reporting process. Finally, in order to improve the assessment of potential economic impact (without compromising research quality), RCUK agreed to increase the level of input from users to the peer review process and to improve guidance for referees and assessors on how to assess impact.

Individual Research Councils have also responded to the outcome of the consultation and pressure on the peer review system. EPSRC, for example, announced in spring 2009 that it would no longer accept uninvited resubmissions of proposals and that from April 2010 it would only allow repeatedly unsuccessful applicants to submit one application in the following 12 months. The new restrictions apply to Principal Investigators who have three or more projects within a two-year period ranked in the bottom half of a funding prioritization list and have an overall personal success rate of less than 25 per cent. Other councils are considering restricting the overall total number of applications that can be submitted in one year at institution level, where particular institutions have consistently low success rates.

The validity of peer review

In parallel with discussions about reducing the burden and increasing the effectiveness of peer review, there has been ongoing discussion in the academic literature about the validity of the process. The selective allocation of funding on the basis of peer review rests on the assumption that it is the best proposals and best researchers who will win out in the competitive process. Indeed, it is assumed that non-quality related conditions and characteristics will not distort decision making to any significant extent. However, there is growing evidence that a proposal's chances of success can be influenced by such factors. For example, there is now good evidence that the ratings that are given to the same proposal by different assessors normally differ from each other – sometimes substantially (e.g. Cicchetti 1991; Wenneras and World 1999). Researchers working in this area often illustrate this variability by referring to the concept of 'single rater reliability'. Marsh and Ball (1991) defined single rater reliability as the correlation between two independent assessors of the same submission across a large number of different submissions. Cicchetti (1991) reported single rater reliabilities between 0.17 and 0.37 (where perfect reliability would be 1.0), based on nine analyses of reviews of National Science Foundation grant submissions in the US.

Peer review of grant applications is not usually carried out 'blind' (i.e. so that assessors are unaware of the identity of the applicant) as assessors typically have to take the applicant's track record into account when making their judgements. Not surprisingly, there has therefore been considerable interest in what characteristics of researchers (such as age, gender, position, institution) and reviewers (such as whether they are nominated by applicants or selected by the funding body) are associated with peer reviewer assessments, and whether these constitute a potential bias in the process. Jayasinghe et al., for example, carried out a number of studies which computed the reliabilities of external reviewer ratings of Australian ARC large grants proposals (e.g. Jayasinghe et al. 2003; Marsh et al. 2007; Marsh et al. 2008). In addition to looking at the effects of age, gender, job position and institution, they assessed whether researcher-nominated reviewers gave systematically higher or otherwise less reliable ratings than ARC nominated ones. They also looked at whether the number of grant applications assessed in a year, or the country of residence of the assessor (Australia or otherwise), made a difference. Overall, their findings showed worryingly low levels of single rater reliability (for example 0.15 for assessments of proposed project and 0.21 for assessments of the research applicant or team). On the basis of this, they determined that it would take at least six assessors per proposal to achieve more acceptable reliability estimates.

In terms of specific characteristics of applicants or assessors, their studies showed no evidence of age or gender bias (in terms of either applicant or reviewer gender), but a significant effect of the applicant's job position (professor or not), and a substantial effect of standing of institution, so that proposals from professors and those in leading institutions scored more highly. Interestingly, ratings by Australian assessors were significantly lower than those made by assessors from other countries. In addition, they found that assessors who were nominated by applicants gave systematically higher scores than did ARC nominated assessors. Finally, they found that proposals that were rated by assessors who reviewed a larger number of applications per year were judged more harshly, but that single rater reliabilities were more valid.

Laudel (2006) identified a number of more general factors that can influence a proposal's chance of success. Thus, he suggested that often neglected factors include the country's general level of investment in research, and the field of research outlined in the proposal. Research fields differ in the amount of money that is available for distribution (often as a result of how it fits in with Government priorities), the costs of the research, and the extent to which the applicant is able to attract collaborators and build a competitive research team. Another factor is the extent to which the applicant has been given time and opportunity by their institution (and their personal situation) to build up a track record. Laudel recommended that institutions can improve the chances of the success of proposals by:

- providing researchers with seedcorn funding so that they can carry out necessary preparatory work;
- providing good administrative support to help with the preparation of grant applications;
- rewarding successful scientists, motivating them to apply for further funding.

If you work within a university, your institution may well incorporate one or more of these measures. There are also many measures that you, as an individual researcher, can take to improve your chances of success when submitting grant applications. These are outlined in the next two chapters, with Chapter 6 being aimed specifically at helping those of you in the early stages of your research career, and Chapter 7 providing useful advice irrespective of your career stage.

6

How to get started

*Formulating a research proposal • Taking the first steps • Different
strategies that can be adopted • Schemes for new researchers
• What constitutes a new researcher?*

If you are at the start of your research career, or have not been involved in
grant getting to date, this chapter provides some helpful advice about how to
get started and provides an overview of funding schemes that are specifically
aimed at new researchers. Those of you who are a little more experienced, but
nevertheless need to improve your grant winning skills, should move on to
Chapter 7.

Starting out in the grant getting business can be a very daunting prospect.
Many new researchers do not know where best to start. You may be in your first
lectureship position and have some ideas for follow-on research stemming
from your thesis or a postdoctoral project, but may not know how to shape
these into grant proposals or where to look for funding. Others of you may
have been working in academia for some years but have not had the opportunity, or motivation, to apply for research funding. You too may have little idea
about how to bring together tentative ideas into a coherent and fundable
proposal.

Formulating a research proposal

So, where do you start? It is virtually always better to start with your ideas for
the research that you would like to carry out, and then think about shaping

these, and formulating them into a possible project, rather than starting by identifying a funding source and then thinking about what you can do that might attract funding from that source. Many new researchers have ideas about a piece of research they would like to conduct, or questions they would like to address, but are either uncertain about, or do not appreciate, what is required to develop these into a truly competitive proposal. A characteristic that is fairly common in researchers who have recently completed PhDs is to assume that a funding body will be happy simply to fund them to continue with this work. For a few lucky applicants, this might be true but, by and large, this is not the case. Many of the ideas for follow-on work at the end of a PhD tend to be rather incremental in nature, often addressing small follow-on questions or tidying up loose ends that may seem really important to you as the applicant but might not seem quite as important to others. However, to be successful, proposals need to take the earlier research to a new level, by addressing new questions, or similar questions in importantly different contexts. Similarly, if you are proposing to carry out some research that follows on from a postdoctoral project that you have worked on (under the guidance of a principal investigator), you will need to show how you are taking the work in a new direction and how you can make an independent contribution to the area in question. An exception to this might be when applying for an early career fellowship (see below). One useful tip when selecting a project topic is to consider what areas of research are seen to be of priority by the various funding organizations. By and large, it should be easier to win funding in these areas than in what might be deemed 'less fashionable' areas. However you should only do this if you have the appropriate expertise and, even more importantly, interest. You will need to convey knowledge about, and enthusiasm for, the proposed research area if you are to stand any chance of success.

It is important to get the scale and scope of projects right. As noted above, you should not plan to carry out minor incremental work that simply follows on from your earlier work, or seek support for a disconnected series of studies. On the other hand, you should not write proposals for projects that 'promise the earth'. A common characteristic of proposals submitted by many new researchers is that they tend to be overly ambitious, trying to do too much and solve all problems, and are not achievable in the timescale and with the resources requested. Discussing ideas with more experienced researchers and looking at examples of successful applications will provide some guidance.

A problem that often occurs in relation to research in the arts and humanities, and some areas of the social sciences, is that new researchers have difficulty shaping their ideas into actual projects that might employ someone else, rather than simply thinking about how to free up their own time so that they can continue to work in pretty much the same way as they did when studying for their PhD. This difficulty is not specific to new researchers. As the pressure on academics to gain external funding for research builds, many arts and humanities scholars, at all levels, are having to grapple with this difficulty. Again, looking at examples of successful project applications can give you ideas about how other researchers frame their research ideas into fundable projects.

Taking the first steps

Whatever the problem, there are a number of ways in which you as a new researcher can start to develop your grant writing and winning skills.

The importance of a good mentor

Having a good mentor is absolutely vital, whether you are a new researcher at the start of your academic career or someone who has been in academia for a while but is refocusing energy towards research and applying for funding. Your mentor must have the appropriate skills and experience to advise you specifically about research. A teaching-focused mentor might be useful when preparing new teaching materials, or for providing comments on your lecturing performance, but might not be the best person to help you develop in your research career. If you are at the start of your academic career, therefore, you may need more than one mentor. As Johnson (2009) points out, the best mentor is often someone who may not be in the same research discipline, or even necessarily the same department or organization. The most important factor is that they are able and willing to provide critical advice on all aspects of career development, including those related to grant getting.

You should discuss your tentative ideas for research (at the earliest stage) with your mentor and get their views on whether the ideas are worth pursuing further. If you are told that your ideas are unlikely to develop into fundable projects then talk to your mentor about what sorts of topics and approach would be more competitive. If your initial ideas show potential, your mentor will be able to advise you on how to shape these into a coherent project, and suggest who else you should talk to, and whether you need a collaborator with specific complementary expertise and skills. They will also be able to help direct you to potential funding sources and may well have knowledge about specific schemes aimed at new researchers. At the later stages, a mentor will be able to comment on draft versions of a proposal and help you to prepare any subsequent response to reviewers. If you are successful in gaining funding they will also be able to advise you about recruiting staff and managing the project, as well as about how best to disseminate your findings appropriately.

The importance of talking to others

Having a good mentor is key but this is not sufficient. You also need to talk to other people about your research ideas. Getting different views from people with different types of expertise and interests is key to shaping your ideas. If you are based in a research group then you should share your early ideas with others in the group. If not, then try to find other opportunities to discuss tentative ideas with colleagues. Once you have drafted a proposal it is particularly important to get feedback from others. This should include someone who has no knowledge of your particular subject area, in addition to feedback from one or more people who have more detailed knowledge. You should remember that grants committees will not be made up solely of people who will have knowledge of your subject area, so any proposal you write must be clear and convincing to intelligent people working in other broad disciplinary areas. It needs to be clear to such people why it is important that the proposed research is carried out, what will be done, how it will be done and what the outcomes and benefits will be (see Chapter 7). Many organizations and departments operate more formal internal peer review systems that proposals have to go through before being submitted, as poor quality applications and low success rates reflect badly on departments and institutions, not just the individual researchers.

Use your university's research development office

Nearly all universities have a section of its administrative services that is responsible for supporting researchers in the grant getting process. This may be called a Research Development or Research Support Office. Staff in such offices typically include people who can help you to identify a funding source, help you complete and submit proposals, and help with drawing up any contracts, and handling post-award accounting matters.

It is normally the case that these people will have knowledge about most mainstream funding organizations and schemes and will have broad experience and ideas about what makes a sound proposal, what might be competitive and what might not, and how to identify what resources you will need, and how to justify these in your proposal. If you are lucky, they will also know whether a proposal reads convincingly and can help with the presentation of your case. They will certainly be able to advise you and help you with the more administrative aspects in terms of preparing budgets and completing forms. With many funding sources, including the Research Councils and major charities, they will have to 'sign off' the proposal and carry out the final submission, as awards are generally made to institutions not to individual researchers.

Read other people's successful proposals

Your university's Research Support Office, or your own department, may well keep copies of successful proposals. If so, then you should read some that are most relevant to your subject area and the type of research you propose to carry out. If not, then ask established researchers in your department if you can read copies of their own previously successful proposals. You will learn a lot about what a good proposal looks like, how it is structured, the length of various sections and the amount of detail included, how arguments are made, and so on. At a higher level, you will get a feel for the size and scale of projects funded under different schemes. If possible, you should also look at copies of unsuccessful proposals to get a feel for what some potential weaknesses might be. In addition to looking at proposals, you should also try to look at examples of successful responses to reviewers' comments, where these are available. Again, a lot can be learned from how these are crafted, the tone that is used, and the way potential criticisms are addressed.

Identifying a suitable funder

You may well get good advice from your mentor, other colleagues, or your institution's research development office, in terms of who would be appropriate to fund your research. However, you can also do some homework yourself. ResearchResearch, for example, is a web based version of the Research Fortnight magazine, that is subscribed to by many institutions. The ResearchResearch website has a helpful electronic guide to funding sources, both within the UK and overseas. The site gives an alphabetical list of all research areas. Clicking on the name of a particular disciplinary area (e.g. abnormal psychology) takes you to a list of potential funders and funding schemes. The COS (Community of Science) database also has detailed information about many government and private international funding opportunities. If you have some idea about a potential funding source, but are not certain, it is often useful to look at a list of projects that have been funded by the organization over the previous year or two. Most major funding bodies publish such information on their websites and in their annual reports. The titles of projects, and the amount of funding awarded, will give you some feel for the sorts of research that the funding organization will support, and may suggest related work that you might want to cite in your literature review.

Do your homework on proposed funding organizations

Once you have a better idea of who might be a potential funder of your research, you should find out as much information about their schemes as possible. Many funding organizations now have exceedingly good websites that provide helpful and comprehensive information. This will include an overview of the organization's aims and remit, and details of their standard funding schemes, as well as of specific initiatives and targeted programmes. You will need to check eligibility criteria to ensure that your proposed project would be suitable for the particular scheme you have in mind, or that you are at the right stage of career. You also need to ensure that the project fits with the overall aims and remit of the scheme. Many of the major funding bodies, including the UK Research Councils, have links to their Research Funding

Guides (often as a downloadable PDF document). Such documents contain very useful information that will help you select a particular scheme and prepare a proposal. The websites also usually list contact names of people responsible for administering the various schemes. If you are uncertain about whether a particular scheme is suitable for your proposed project (or for you as an individual), then contact the named person and ask their advice. Finally, as pointed out in Chapter 5, in order to write a competitive proposal, you will need to be aware of the specific criteria that will be used to assess it. Again, in many cases, this information is available on funders' websites.

Attend relevant training sessions and other relevant briefings and roadshows

Many institutions will provide training sessions (sometimes as part of their new lecturers' course) on applying for research funding. It is worth signing up for one of these sessions. In addition, research funders themselves now make an effort to get out into the community in order to inform researchers about their various schemes. Some funding organizations make visits to institutions, others organize regional roadshows, or run dedicated sessions at events organized by professional subject associations. At such meetings, you will hear up-to-date information about recent funding opportunities, and will have an opportunity to meet and talk to key staff. There are also some commercially run training sessions. The Missenden Centre for the Development of Higher Education, for example, runs several sessions a year on how to make a successful research grant proposal. More details can be found on their website.

Making time for research

To say that you need to make time for research, and for applying for funding, may seem obvious, but it is important that you do organize your time effectively. It is all too easy to keep delaying writing a grant application on the grounds that there is never enough 'quality' or uninterrupted time. It is often difficult for new researchers, in particular, who may be simultaneously producing their first lecture courses, attending professional training sessions, and often carrying out teaching-related administration for the first time. At this stage of career, the weeks have the habit of flying past, with many good intentions not being realized. It is therefore important to try to block out some dedicated time for grant writing. Ideally this should be at least one day per week when you have no other duties, but could be two or three separate half days. Put a line through your diary on these 'blocked out' times and be strict about not agreeing to do anything else in this time. There are ways in which teaching and other tasks can be organized in order to facilitate time management. Many institutions, for example, have moved to a 'team-teaching' approach, where several members of staff contribute to a particular course, enabling more flexibility. You should discuss the organization of teaching, if relevant to your position, with your mentor or head of teaching. Another tip is to make sure that you use smaller amounts of time effectively. If you have an additional hour between other commitments, do not feel that it is too short a time to do anything worthwhile. There are usually some parts of the grant application process that can be carried out even in smaller chunks of time. This might include searching for and compiling references for bibliographies, updating CVs, and getting quotations for equipment or other budgetary information. This allows you to use the unbroken 'quality' time for activities that require more dedicated thinking time, such as planning programmes of work, designing studies and writing introductory and background sections of proposals.

Staying relatively focused

Related to the above issue is the need to use available time productively in a way that will deliver and enable you to establish a successful track record. Some new researchers have a tendency to try to engage in too many research projects and collaborations, with the aim of keeping options open and increasing chances of success, but often with the effect of not delivering appropriately on any one front. It is important to stay relatively focused in the early stages, to enable you to 'gain some depth' and start to establish a track record and reputation in a particular area.

Different strategies that can be adopted

Many new researchers adopt one of two general strategies when starting out in the grant getting business. The first, 'lone researcher' model is to start out by applying for small amounts of money to carry out pilot or preliminary projects. The British Academy and Nuffield Foundation, for example, both run schemes that offer support up to a maximum of £7500 (see below). These schemes enable you to develop a track record and put you in a stronger position to gain more substantial funding. Similarly, the Royal Society has a scheme where new researchers can apply for funding to purchase an essential piece of equipment (up to £15000), again enabling you to start to progress your research before applying for project funding.

If a larger amount of funding is needed to support the proposed project (which is often the case in many areas of the sciences), many funding organizations (including most of the UK Research Councils) run schemes that are specifically aimed at new researchers (see below). Most of these put an upper limit on the amount of funding that can be applied for, and have specific criteria to govern who is eligible to benefit from the scheme.

Winning one or more small grants in the early career stage enables new researchers to build up a track record so that they will then be in a position to compete on a more equal footing with more established researchers. Small grants can therefore be helpful to allow you to 'get on the funding ladder' or to prove a principle, but you need to be sure that they will meet your objectives and not overly constrain your plans and activities, and that the benefit of getting the award will not be outweighed by any onerous reporting requirements or bureaucratic procedures.

Another strategy that can be used by new researchers is the 'collaborator' model. In this case, a new researcher is initially teamed up with a more experienced researcher (in the same or related area) and works on a proposal that the more experienced researcher is developing. The new researcher benefits from the learning experience, and starts to gain a track record by being a co-applicant on the project. This model is often used when new researchers join larger, more established, research groups.

Deciding which of these two routes to go down will depend on your research area, the minimum cost of any support you will need to carry out a worthwhile pilot study or small project, and the availability of suitable collaborators. If you can usefully conduct a small scale pilot study that will provide useful data for a few thousand pounds then the former route might be a more effective way to get started, particularly if well inclined collaborators are not immediately at hand.

Schemes for new researchers

New researchers who, by definition, will not have proven track records would normally find it difficult to compete for research funding on equal terms with more experienced researchers. A study carried out in relation to the Australian Research Council (ARC) by Bazeley (2003) found that applicants who win ARC large project grants have a strong publication record, have a history of involvement in previous ARC grants, and are either of full professorial status or collaborating with someone who is, or in a research-only position. Bazeley noted that, without an established track record in attracting funding and, as yet, unknown in the research community, new investigators are less able to match esteemed researchers for support in highly competitive schemes.

As a result of such concerns, many research funders (including the UK Research Councils) have established funding schemes that are aimed specifically at newer researchers. The primary aim of such schemes is to help early career researchers to establish a track record so that they can compete in standard funding competitions on an equal footing with more experienced researchers. When judging proposals, funding committees take account of research potential, as opposed to previous track record.

New Researcher Research Grants schemes

A number of funding schemes have been established to help early career researchers to gain their first research grants. EPSRC, for example, runs a first grants scheme to help new academics at the start of their career. Such academics can only apply for a first grant once, whether or not the proposal is successful. This means it is important to ensure that the proposal is as strong as it can be when it is submitted. As we will see later, many new researchers are tempted to 'rush' their proposals and do not appreciate the time it will take to develop one that is likely to be successful. To be eligible for the scheme, you must have been appointed to your first academic position in a UK university within the previous 36 months and must hold a university position that includes lecturing and administrative responsibilities as well as research. If you hold a research-only contract or you are employed wholly by a Research Council establishment you will not be eligible; nor are applicants who are new to the UK but taking up senior academic positions. To be eligible, you must also have completed a PhD, or equivalent professional qualification, within 10 years of the time you submit the proposal. Funding is capped at a maximum of £125000, and projects are limited to a maximum duration of two years. Applications can be submitted at any time during the year.

BBSRC's equivalent scheme is similar but involves slightly different eligibility criteria and levels of support. NERC's scheme is similar again but only offers funding up to a maximum of £40000 for directly incurred costs (see Chapter 9 for an explanation of what this means).

EPSRC also runs a Challenging Engineering scheme for researchers who have established some track record but who are nevertheless still within 10 years of gaining their PhD. The funding (which is frequently over £1 million per award) is intended to support individuals who show real potential as future research leaders and to help them to develop their own research groups rather than fund project based proposals. Calls are normally issued annually, and there is a two-stage assessment process. In the first stage, a panel of experts shortlist applicants based on criteria described in the call and fit to the initiative's aims. In the second phase, applicants are invited to an assessment day, which includes an open session with the panel and an interview. This is a highly competitive scheme, so only the strongest applicants should apply.

The MRC's new investigator scheme is similarly competitive, and researchers who are successful, while being relatively early in career, have nevertheless already published a number of strong outputs and have, usually, previously gained some research funding. To be eligible, you must be based at a UK institution and hold a PhD or MD, and should either be at the start of your first academic appointment or be in a senior postdoctoral position and have between three and ten years' postdoctoral research experience. If you do not hold a 'permanent' position, your host organization will have to provide written confirmation that it will seriously consider you for a permanent position during the lifetime of the award. MRC new investigator awards provide funding (up to a maximum of £600000) for three years and are not renewable. The scheme is for sole applicants only, although other researchers can be named as collaborators.

For those of you working in the arts and humanities, AHRC has introduced a route for early career researchers as part of their standard research grants scheme. Again it is aimed at assisting new researchers at the start of their careers in gaining experience of managing and leading research projects. Applications may be submitted for proposals costing between £20 000 and £200 000 and for a duration of up to 60 months. To be eligible for the scheme, you should not have already been a principal applicant/investigator on an AHRC funded project, and should be within six years of your first academic appointment (or within eight years of award of PhD or equivalent professional training).

Finally, unlike the other Research Councils, ESRC does not run a grants scheme that is specifically aimed at new researchers. However, as part of its standard research grants scheme, ESRC runs a small grants competition (for projects costing between £15 000 and £99 999). The competition is open to all researchers but is particularly suited to those who are early in their career. The assessment process for the small grants scheme is more streamlined and typically faster (normally taking less than 14 weeks) than for the standard research grants scheme. Applications do not go to the full meetings of the Grants Board but instead are assessed by a member of the Grants Board and a member of the Virtual College, who advise the Board Chair (or Deputy Chair), who makes a funding recommendation. ESRC has also introduced a new scheme to boost international mobility, exchange and networking for early career researchers. The New International Activities for Early Career Researchers scheme aims to support established international networks and activities, or the development of new activities based on clear evidence of need or demand. Activities may include the provision of international workshops, summer schools, or other events that stimulate networking around shared research or methodological agendas, short-term mobility opportunities to engage researchers to participate in international events or benefit from facilities or expertise only available outside the UK. The scheme is open to postgraduate research students and researchers within five years of completion of their PhD. Awards are made up to a maximum of £40 000.

Three other schemes are particularly worthy of mention, even though the maximum amount of funding in each case is relatively low. These are the British Academy, Nuffield Foundation and Royal Society small grants schemes, which were briefly described in the previous chapter. As far as the British Academy's scheme is concerned, applications for individual or collaborative projects are welcome, and funds are available to facilitate initial project planning and development, to support the direct costs of research, and to enable the advancement of research through workshops or visits. Applicants must have a PhD, but do not need to hold a permanent position in a UK institution. There are usually two funding rounds a year. Applicants for the Nuffield scheme must have a permanent contract or a research contract of three years or more at a UK institution, although the research may be undertaken outside the UK. Applications can be made at any time of year. Finally, the Royal Society's Research Grants scheme provides seedcorn funding, of up to £15000, for new researchers to purchase specialized equipment, essential consumable materials and services, and to support essential field research. The scheme also provides support for research in the history of science. Applicants must be of postdoctoral status and within the first five years of the start date of their first permanent academic appointment. There are two funding rounds per year.

Although the amount of funding available in these schemes is relatively small, it can be sufficient to enable you to carry out a project that results in a strong research output or a body of data that confirms the appropriateness of a particular technique, or to purchase a piece of equipment that is central to your research, in each case putting you in a stronger position to secure subsequent funding. The Nuffield scheme, for example, might be appropriate if you want to determine whether a particular procedure (such as eye tracking) is suitable for use with children suffering from a particular disorder, and to investigate how such children process sentences compared with typically developing children. Similarly, the British Academy scheme might be appropriate if you want to conduct field research at a United Nations office in the United States for a writers' workshop to produce an edited volume.

Fellowship schemes for early career researchers

Many funding organizations also run specific fellowship schemes aimed at those in the early stages of their career. As noted in Chapter 3, a research fellowship may be a more appropriate form of funding if developing your research career is a primary aim rather than carrying out a specific, well-formulated, project. Some fellowship schemes will simply cover your personal salary but others offer different degrees of additional support. EPSRC's postdoctoral fellowships scheme, for example, is aimed at enabling new researchers to establish an independent research career shortly, or immediately, after completing a PhD. Funding is provided to cover the Fellow's salary and a small amount of travel and subsistence, equipment and consumables. Fellowships normally last for three years. There is an annual closing date, which differs for the different programme areas. NERC's equivalent scheme also makes early career development awards of up to three years. The scheme is open to those of you who have just completed your PhD, but some post-doctoral experience is said to be an advantage (between one and five years). ESRC's postdoctoral fellowship scheme, in contrast, only funds new researchers for one year immediately after submission of their doctorate. Those of you with more experience should apply through their standard Research Fellowship Scheme.

Both MRC and BBSRC's fellowship schemes for new researchers expect applicants to have a minimum of three years postdoctoral experience. Upper limits are six and ten years for the MRC Career Development Awards and BBSRC David Phillips Fellowships, respectively. Both schemes provide five years' funding to cover the cost of salary as well as a significant amount of research support. Both schemes are highly competitive, and it is only worth submitting an application if you have a relatively strong track record for your stage of career.

Finally, as far as the Research Councils are concerned, AHRC has established a new Research Fellowships scheme that has a strand aimed specifically at new researchers. Length of awards varies between three and nine months, and award holders must dedicate between 50 per cent and 100 per cent of their time to the Fellowship. To be eligible to apply, you should have between one and eight years' postdoctoral research experience. Funding is provided so that you can pursue new avenues of research, developed since completion of your PhD. Applications must be accompanied by a letter of support from the host institution, outlining what support will be provided to develop your research career, including details of proposed mentoring arrangements.

In addition to the UK Research Councils, many of the larger charities and trusts provide funding to support research fellowships, including the Wellcome Trust, British Academy and Leverhulme Trust. Details of eligibility criteria and types and levels of support available can be found on the funders' websites.

What constitutes a new researcher?

One thing that becomes apparent from looking at the different eligibility criteria of the various schemes is that the different funding organizations tend to employ slightly different criteria to define what counts as a new researcher. Interestingly, when the Australian Research Council decided to set up a scheme aimed at supporting new researchers, they carried out a prior study to determine what characteristics stand out as being essential for success as an early career researcher. They identified two such criteria: adequate research training and experience (evidenced by having a PhD and publications) and security of employment from which one might build a research programme and apply for funding. It was noted that motivation was also an important component (Bazeley 2003). ARC ended up by defining an early career researcher as 'one who is currently within their first five years of academic or other research-related employment, allowing uninterrupted, stable research development following the complement of postgraduate research training' (Bazeley 2003). The definition assumes that completion of such training is an essential foundation on which to build, and that five years is sufficient time in which to begin to build a track record, assuming stability of employment sufficient to allow development of a personal research programme.

It should be noted that schemes for new researchers are normally aimed at researchers who are relatively early on in their postdoctoral phase (e.g. have completed a PhD within the past 10 years) or are in their first three years of academic employment. Most of the definitions that are employed would exclude researchers who have been in academic positions for a longer period of time, but have not had the opportunity or motivation to apply for research funding in the past.

7

Characteristics of a winning proposal

Choosing your topic • Searching the literature • Identifying what is needed to support the proposed research • Establishing a research team • Selecting a funder and studying their guidelines • Familiarizing yourself with the assessment criteria • Soliciting help and feedback • Structuring a proposal • Preparing a case for support • Nominating referees • Presenting your case clearly and convincingly • Deciding when it's ready to submit • Submitting your proposal • Responding to reviewers • Preparing for interviews • Coping with rejection • Coping with success

We have already noted that gaining funding for research has become an increasingly competitive process. To be successful, you will need to ensure that any proposals you submit are of the highest quality. This involves both having good ideas and presenting these clearly and convincingly. Even potentially the strongest ideas are unlikely to be supported if they are expressed and packaged poorly. Referees and members of grants committees are inevitably busy people, who may well have a very large number of proposals to consider at any one time. Your proposal needs to be well presented, precise and memorable, and should convey your enthusiasm for the project. Successful proposals are those that are distinguishable from the competition (in a positive way). This chapter is aimed at helping you to prepare competitive proposals, in terms of shaping, structuring and presenting your ideas. It should also help you to avoid some of the common weaknesses and mistakes that are associated with unsuccessful applications.

Although this chapter is headed 'Characteristics of a winning proposal', it might be worth starting out with a list of characteristics of unsuccessful proposals, based on one proposed by Ries and Leukefeld (1998). All of the points in the list are picked up in the sections that follow:

- science is either not significant or not original;
- unacceptable/unclear scientific rationale;
- unfocused research plan;
- insufficient amount of methodological detail;
- not experienced in essential methodology;
- unrealistic approach;
- overly ambitious;
- unaware of relevant related work;
- uncertainty about future directions.

Choosing your topic

The research grant application process begins long before you actually start to put words on paper, identify a funding source and complete application forms. It begins with you coming up with sound ideas for a coherent and potentially fundable project or programme of work. As Chapter 6 acknowledges, this process can present particular challenges for those who are new to the grant getting business. However, even for those of you with a little more experience and track record, it is usually best to start out by drawing up a brief outline of your ideas, so that you can test them out on yourself and others. Even from reading a brief outline, it should be clear whether the proposed research is important, novel, sound and will benefit others and appeal to funding bodies. Ideally the proposed research should follow on from previous work that you have done (although not in some simple incremental way) and feed into your overall research strategy. Carrying out a series of isolated and disconnected projects is not usually the best way to build a research career. You should resist chasing potential research grants in a haphazard way, simply responding to funding opportunities. As Gitlin and Lyons (2008) note, 'writing a grant should be part of a research career trajectory' (p. 15). It is also important for you to want to carry out the proposed research and feel real enthusiasm for the subject.

Searching the literature

Once you have decided on your research topic, and the question or questions you would like to address, it is important to conduct a literature search in order to determine what related research has already been conducted and published, and to ensure that no one has already published your intended study. Searching the academic literature is relatively easy these days, given access to publication databases such as the ISI Web of Knowledge. The Web of Knowledge service provides a single route of access to Thomson Reuter's products, including the Web of Science (which covers the Science Citation Index, Social Science Citation Index, Arts and Humanities Citation Index, and the Conference Proceedings Citation Index) and Medline. Other commonly used databases include PubMed (for health and medical related outputs) and WorldCat (which covers published books). There are also a number of single discipline based databases, such as PsychLit (which covers the psychology research literature).

To search such databases, it is necessary to identify a number of appropriate search terms. Given the vast amount of material in the databases it is important that relatively restrictive search terms are used, including, for example, specifying how many years' worth of publications you want the search to cover. The search engine will list details of relevant publications and usually provide a link to the abstract or summary. Reading these should give you a good idea of whether or not the publication is relevant to your project and whether you want to access the full text. You can also see the number of times each article has been cited, and by whom, providing you with a source of potential further relevant publications. Other ways of identifying relevant publications include using Google Scholar, and World Cat and the Amazon website for books.

Once you know which publications you would like to read in more detail, you need to access the full texts. You may be able to gain access to some of these electronically, either free of charge or in return for a payment to the publisher. Whether or not they are available free of charge will depend on which electronic publications your institution subscribes to and the access policies of particular publishers. If you know the author's institution, it is also worth checking to see if publications are available on the author's personal website or in the institution's publications repository. When publications are not available electronically, and are not held in your own institutional library, you may be able to request copies through the inter library loan service that your library will support. Finally, for some areas of research, you may need to access more specialist libraries and collections that are based elsewhere and will usually require you to read the materials in situ. It is sometimes necessary to book such access in advance.

Identifying what is needed to support the proposed research

At an early stage you will need to think about what is needed to support the research that you want to conduct. Can you do it alone or do you need one or more collaborators with complementary expertise? If so, are such people based in your own institution or do you have to look further afield? Do you already have the right contacts and relationships or do these need to be developed? If the latter is the case, then you need to appreciate that this often takes time, and that marriages of convenience rarely result in successful proposals. A successful and productive collaboration usually results from researchers coming together who not only have complementary expertise but are also able to work together and 'get on well', at least to some extent. You may also need to consider whether you need access to specific participant populations or materials in order to carry out the project. If so, have you secured such access and can you convince funders that what you propose is feasible? Similarly, does your proposed project require the use of specialized equipment or other infrastructure that cannot be considered for funding as part of the project and, if so, do you have, or can you arrange, access to such equipment? You will also need to consider how long the project would take to complete, and what specific resources (staffing and others) would be needed to carry it out, so that you can start to identify a potential funder and funding scheme that would be appropriate. Chapter 9 looks in more detail at how to determine the specific resources that you will need to carry out your proposed project.

Establishing a research team

If you do not have all of the necessary skills and expertise to be a sole applicant, you will need to involve others. Gitlin and Lyons (2008) outline three different models according to which this might be done. In the Consultative model, the principal investigator (PI) develops the project idea and then requests assistance from experts or consultants who can contribute specific expertise or skills that they do not possess. If you are involving such consultants in your project, you will need to make it clear in your application what their role will be and how they will support the project. In the Cooperative model, the lead researcher identifies the idea for the project and then invites one or more other researchers to work on specific aspects of it. According to Gitlin and Lyons the model is effective in projects involving multiple and distinct tasks, clear division of labour and distinct work performed by each participating person or group.

Finally, the Collaborative model builds on the Cooperative model, and involves a more complex structure. It relies on the development of a team that will work on all, or most, aspects of the project, rather than specific members working on specific aspects. Although collaborative teams may have different complementary skills, they share a commitment to a common purpose or mutual goal. Gitlin and Lyons (2008) propose that a good working collaboration involves experts working together in such a way as to build on each other's strengths, backgrounds and experience, so that an integrative approach to the research problem is achieved. Each person combines their skills with those of other team members in such a way that problems may be redefined and solutions found that reflect multiple levels of expertise and knowledge. The final project plan then represents the integration of multiple perspectives and is the product of group interaction.

There may well be occasions in your career when, rather than being the lead applicant who is looking for potential project partners, you are approached by another researcher leader who wants you to participate in his or her project. Gitlin and Lyons suggest that, when considering whether or not to engage in such collaborations, researchers need to ask themselves the following three questions:

• Will I benefit from participating in this group?
• Can I satisfy the group's requirements?
• Are the benefits offered by the participation worth the effort?

It is advisable only to join the team if the answer to the above three questions is 'yes'. In general, it is better to be involved in a small number of very productive collaborations than a large number of ones that are of relatively little value and risk distracting you from other more important things. It is also important to realize that although many good collaborations may last for years and continue to be productive, some may only be productive for a relatively short time. You should not be afraid to let collaborations that cease to be productive wither.

Selecting a funder and studying their guidelines

Experienced researchers are likely to know who their potential funders are, and what schemes are available to support different types of research. Newer researchers are likely to need help to identify one or more potential funding source and appropriate schemes. As outlined in Chapter 6, research mentors and staff in university research support offices can be very helpful here. Whatever your stage of career, it is essential to do detailed homework on your potential funding body or bodies. Funders are continuously revising and updating their schemes, and rules and regulations that were in place when you submitted an application a couple of years ago may no longer be in place. You should always ensure that you are using the most recent versions of guidelines and application forms.

First and foremost, you need to ensure that your proposed research fits with the overall aims and remit of the potential funder. If you are preparing a responsive mode application, you will need to ensure that it falls within (and is preferably a core part of) the areas of research that are supported by the organization in order to fulfil its mission. If you are submitting an application to be considered as part of a more directed funding programme, you will need to ensure that what you are proposing fits with the main objectives and desired approaches of the specific programme. You will also need to ensure that the scope and scale of your proposed project is in line with the targeted funding scheme. There is no point in preparing a bid for a five year programme if the scheme only funds smaller project grants, or preparing one that will cost £1.2 million when the maximum funding limit is £400 000. Similarly, there is no point in preparing a strong standalone project grant for a scheme that only supports larger multidisciplinary consortia.

Second, you need to seek out, and study, the most up-to-date information on the proposed funding source and funding schemes. In many cases this is now available on the internet. You need to check that you are eligible to apply to the particular scheme you have in mind and that it will fund the resources that you need to complete your project. Many of the major funding bodies produce detailed Research Funding Guides that are usually available as PDF documents on their websites. It is advisable to download these and read through them in detail. Most funding bodies will also produce specific guidance for applicants in terms of what information is needed, and how it should be structured on the application form. Again, it is essential to comply with such guidance.

As pointed out in Chapter 6, another useful tip if you have not applied to a particular funding organization, or for a specific scheme, before is to look at what projects they have funded over the previous year or two, if this information is available. Most of the larger funding organizations will publish lists of previously awarded grants on their websites and in annual reports. Reading such lists will give you a feel for the specific areas in which they have supported research in the recent past. Another tip is to try to read examples of successful proposals that have previously been funded by the organization under the scheme you have in mind. This will enable you to learn a lot about what sort of research is funded, the size and scope of projects, and how ideas can be presented convincingly. Some research support offices keep libraries of such proposals. If yours does not, then ask colleagues whom you know have previously submitted successful bids.

If you have any doubts at all about whether a particular scheme is suitable for you, and whether it will support what you want to do, then consul one of the research officers in the funding organization. Contact names are normally provided on the organizations' websites. These people will be very experienced at talking to researchers about potential projects, whether these fall within the remit and scope of the schemes they support, and what might or might not be a competitive proposal. It is particularly important to talk to such people at an early stage in your thinking if you are wanting support for a larger programme, network, or centre, or for a more advanced fellowship. It is in the funders' interest to encourage high quality proposals that are appropriate for their schemes, so they will be happy to talk to you. In the case of directed research programmes, the programme director or coordinator can also be a useful source of advice and guidance. These individuals are typically academics who have been seconded from their institution, for all or part of their time, so that they can direct the programme throughout its duration. You should not, however, contact members of grants committees to ask their advice, particularly if you do not know them well. Such people need to remain, and be seen to remain, impartial.

If you are considering applying for EU funding, and are based within the UK, UKRO is a much better, and easier to access, source of information than the European Commission itself. The UKRO website is also more helpful than the official EU website (Community Research and Development Information Service, CORDIS). There are also national contact points for individual themes in the main Cooperation programme, and for the Marie Curie programme, and the European Research Council, and these people can be approached for further advice. One useful tip is to sign up to be an evaluator, so that you get more experience about how successful proposals are constructed and managed. Engagement in an EU funding bid may well require you to attend meetings (outside the UK) with potential partners in order to put together a competitive bid. There are a number of sources of funding that can be accessed to support such travel, including the EPSRC Overseas Travel Grants, BBSRC International Scientific Exchange Scheme, and the Royal Society and British Academy.

Finally, before investing too much time in any application, you need to consider what your chances of success are likely to be, given the funding scheme in question, and weigh these up against the amount of time and effort that would be needed to prepare a successful application. In some cases, where schemes are highly competitive or when deadlines are short and the likelihood of preparing a convincing application is limited, it may be better not to apply and to look for an alternative funding source. You should also never try to distort a particular funding scheme to suit your particular application and needs, or distort your application to make it appear as if it fits the scheme, when in practice it does not. Many proposals are unsuccessful simply because they have been submitted to the wrong scheme. You should remember that it reflects badly on you and your institution if you establish a poor success rate by repeatedly rushing proposals or submitting applications to inappropriate schemes.

Familiarizing yourself with the assessment criteria

In order to write a competitive proposal it is important that you know the criteria by which it will be assessed. Again, many funding organizations publish these in their funding guides and on their websites. If you are unable to find these, then contact the organization and ask if they can let you have such information, or ask a colleague who you know has acted as a referee for the funding body in question. Chapter 5 outlines the main assessment criteria that are used by some of the major research funders. You can see that many funding schemes use very similar criteria, but you should not assume that the same criteria will automatically apply. Directed programmes, in particular, often have additional criteria by which proposals will be evaluated. As noted in Chapter 5, one way to become familiar with the review criteria and assessment process, and also see a wider set of examples of proposals, is to become a peer reviewer for one or more funding organization. Although acting as a reviewer takes time, it does have its rewards. Through seeing examples of well presented, strongly argued cases for support, and the converse of this, you should get more of a feel for what makes a successful proposal.

Soliciting help and feedback

As noted above, talking to other people about your ideas and project plans is essential throughout the grant getting process. At the earliest stage, you should map out an outline of your ideas and present these either to your mentor or other colleagues. If you work as part of a research group, it is often helpful to present your ideas for funding to the group in a relatively informal way in order to solicit their feedback and to help you shape and refine your ideas. You should then work these ideas up into a longer scientific case or proposal and again seek feedback and advice from colleagues. If your bid forms part of a larger, team based proposal, then you will need to share your specific ideas with other team members to ensure that what you are proposing is in line with the overall scope of the proposed work, and complements the ideas of others in the team. Once you have identified a suitable funding source and scheme, and have completed a draft version of the application, you will need to get feedback on how well you have presented your case. At this stage it is essential to get feedback from one or more people outside your subject area in addition to those with subject specific knowledge. As noted in Chapter 5, grants committees are unlikely to be made up of people who will have specific knowledge of your subject area, so any proposal you write must be clear and convincing to intelligent people working in other broad disciplinary areas. It needs to be clear to such people why it is important that the proposed research is carried out, what will be done, how it will be done, and what the benefits will be. Thus, getting input from non-specialists is just as important as getting input from those with more specialist knowledge.

As indicated in the previous chapter, another helpful source of advice will be your institution's research support office. In addition to handling the more bureaucratic aspects relating to form filling and submission, staff in these offices will usually be able to give you valuable advice about how to formulate your bid, and should give helpful feedback on draft cases for support. You should contact these people at an early stage of your thinking, particularly if you are new to the grant getting process. As a formality, you need to establish whether your institution will accept the award if you are successful. You also need to find out how long they will need to 'sign off' the application. Many such offices require proposals to be submitted to them at least a week before any external deadline. You will also need to consult with your head of department to ensure that your department is willing to host the research and can provide the necessary support, and many application forms will require their signature to confirm this.

Structuring a proposal

Some funding organizations will require applications to conform to a set structure, using particular headings and sub-headings. Others may leave the applicant more freedom to structure the proposal in a way that best suits the particular project. Most proposals, however, are made up of a number of standard sections that can be thought of as a series of questions: what you are proposing to do, why this is important, how you will do it, what is needed for you to do it and how much this will cost, why you are an appropriate person to carry out the research, how you will disseminate your findings and what benefits they will have. ESRC, for example, recommends that when writing applications you need to bear in mind the following:

* What is the story you are telling?
* Who are the audience?
* Why does it matter?
* Why now?
* Why you?

Some application forms will require a number of set questions to be answered, in addition to requiring applicants to produce a fuller case for support. These questions may ask for information about the applicant's previous track record (in the form of a short CV or longer textual summary) and the suitability of the host organization. Several of the Research Councils, for example, now ask applicants to provide a summary of their previous track record (including relevant publications) and to comment on the suitability of the host organization, before describing the proposed research project. Box 7.1 gives an example of what might be included in such statements. Other questions may ask about relevance for beneficiaries and plans for dissemination, and so on. You may also be asked to produce a summary of the proposed research that is specifically aimed at the lay reader. It is important to understand the purpose of each of these questions, or sections, and what material you need to include or cover in your response to each. If word limits are given, it is very important that you do not exceed these as, if you do, your proposal is likely to be returned to you by the funding organization.

Box 7.1 An example of a Previous Track Record summary and statement on suitability of host organization

Dr xxxxxxxx has been a lecturer in the Department of Informatics and Computing at the University of Berkshire since October 2006. She was previously a Research Assistant working with Professor xxxxxx at the Institute for Advanced Study in the Abraham Lincoln University (US), where she co-supervised a project and two PhD students on topics relating to the present proposal. Her academic qualifications include a PhD from the University of Cambridge (UK) and a BSc in mathematics from the University of Bonn. She was awarded the Computational Neurosciences Association prize for the best research output based on doctoral studies published in 2004.

Dr xxxxxxx's research interests focus on the investigation of the encoding and processing of temporal information in the brain. As part of her doctoral studies, she developed a novel system of interacting Markov chains, which was published in the Proceedings of IEEE.

During her time at the Abraham Lincoln University, Dr xxxx worked in the internationally renowned Computational Neurodynamics Group, under the supervision of Professor Susan Shaw. The present research proposal builds on some of the ground breaking research that she and Professor Shaw carried out on the relationship between neurone morphology and response. Dr xxxxx has presented her research at three major international conferences (including the International Conference on Complex Systems, Melbourne 2005, and Computational Neurosciences and Neurodynamics, Peking 2006), and has published a total of seven journal articles, as detailed below. All but one are relevant for the current proposal.

Host institution

The Department of Informatics and Computing at the University of Berkshire has a long standing tradition in computer vision research and the investigation of information processing systems. The Neurodynamics research group (of which Dr xxxxxx is a member) conducts research on novel information processing methods including machine learning approaches to pattern recognition and classification. The group, and the wider department, will provide a supportive environment for the proposed research. The Department has 40 research active staff and a large PhD student cohort, and first class facilities for conducting research. It was awarded a 5* rating in the 2001 Research Assessment Exercise. It routinely attracts a number of visiting professors and other researchers from across the world, adding to the richness of the research environment.

As outlined in Chapter 5, all of the Research Councils now require applicants to produce an 'impact summary' and an 'impact planning statement' in addition to the standard academic summary statement. Impact is interpreted in its broadest sense to embrace the many diverse ways in which research can benefit individuals, organizations and nations, including fostering economic competitiveness, increasing the efficacy of public services and policy, and enhancing quality of life, health and creative output. The impact summary must address three questions: who will benefit from the research (e.g. companies, policy makers, museums, schools, the wider public); how they will benefit (e.g. improved policy making, improvements to healthcare services); and what will be done to ensure they benefit (covering communication and engagement plans, plans for exploitation where appropriate, and so on). The impact plan must describe how the potential impacts of the research will be realized, and expand on your answers to the three questions in the impact planning statement. Several of the Research Councils, particularly EPSRC and ESRC, provide very helpful guides to writing impact summaries and impact planning statements, and address a number of frequently asked questions on their websites, which are definitely worth looking at. They also provide reassurance that excellent research without obvious or immediate impact will not be disadvantaged in the assessment process. However, you would need to justify any 'non-applicable' response to the request for an impact plan in a way that is sufficiently convincing to reviewers and assessors.

Preparing a case for support

Irrespective of any specific questions on the form, most key funding organizations will require you to produce a full case for support, or description of the proposed research. There will usually be a word or page limit for this case (often in the region of six pages, unless a very large programme of work is being described). As noted above, it is essential that you read the detailed application guidelines that will specify exactly what is required, and keep within the word limit. Not complying with these guidelines will result in your proposal being returned to you. When writing your case for support, you need to bear in mind what the research funder will be looking for when selecting applications for funding. Chapter 5 outlines some of the detailed review criteria used by several of the major funders. In general, however, they will be looking for high quality, innovative research, that is significant, timely and internationally competitive. Bushaway (2003) summarizes the key aspects in the following ten key points:

- novel/innovative research;
- sound ideas backed up by knowledge;
- well-contextualized research projects with clear direction;
- appropriate methodology;
- appropriate expertise/track record or access to the right 'know-how';
- research that meets the sponsor's aims and remit;
- evidence of the value of research outputs to the wider audience (including users and beneficiaries);
- evidence that research will be well managed;
- evidence of likely research outcomes;
- value for money – appropriate scale and means.

Typical section headings that may be given on application forms, or you may choose to use when writing the main case for support, are as follows.

Title

The title should succinctly describe the proposed research in a way that informs assessors and others of the topic and nature of the application. Many funders will place an upper limit on the number of words (or often characters) that can be used. If a title is too short, however, it is unlikely to be sufficiently informative. Thus, a title such as 'Human memory' is insufficient, whereas something like 'Investigating the relationship between implicit and explicit memory in children' would be much more appropriate. On the other hand, a title such as 'A cross-sectional study to investigate the relationship between implicit and explicit memory in children aged 3, 5, 7, and 9 years old, using a combination of word completion tasks and cued recall' is too detailed.

Abstract or short summary

This is a brief description of the proposed research (often just a few sentences). It should say, in a nutshell, what you are proposing to do and the methodology you will use. The summary must be concise and comprehensive. It is important that you get this right, as it is often the first part of a grant application that an assessor will read (and will shape their views of what is to follow). It will also be read by all members of grants committees (whereas some of the more detailed information might not be), and will aid office staff in the selection of appropriate referees and assessors. Above all, the summary needs to be attention catching, so that your proposal stands out from the large number of others that may be being considered at the same time. Box 7.2 shows an example of an appropriately worded short summary statement. Three other examples are given in Appendix 8.

Box 7.2 Example of an appropriate abstract/short summary statement

This research is concerned with establishing the extent to which the mere exposure effect should be considered to be an implicit memory phenomenon. First, it addresses a number of currently unresolved differences between the findings in the two literatures. Second, the research examines the processes underlying the mere exposure effect as well as the necessary conditions for obtaining it. The findings will permit an assessment of whether implicit memory and mere exposure effects are subserved by similar systems/processes. More generally, the research should provide a more ecologically valid measure of implicit memory which will benefit investigations of the phenomenon in the real world.

Introduction

Most proposals will begin with an introductory paragraph that sets out the main purpose of the research, why it is important that it is conducted, and at this point in time, and what will be gained if it is funded. The rationale for, and significance of, the proposed research should be clear from reading this section. It should set the stage for what is to come, and lead into the more specific aims and objectives. It is important not to overstate the significance of the project. Do not make exaggerated claims in the hope of impressing referees and assessors. Statements about significance must be objective and related to aims. Getting this introductory paragraph right is vitally important as, like the short summary statement, it will shape assessors' views of what is to follow. An unfocused or unclear introductory paragraph is likely to bias reviewers and assessors against the proposal from the outset. When writing this section (and elsewhere), you should quote the funding organization's literature back to them, making it clear how your ideas map on to their mission and priorities. Having drafted this section, you should ask yourself the following:

- Have I formulated the problem clearly and concisely?
- Have I put it in context of current theoretical debates, and demonstrated the

way the work will build on existing research and make a novel contribution to the area?
- Is there a clear and convincingly argued analytic framework?
- Have I clearly explained what the research will do, and why, and what the benefits will be?

Aims and objectives

As noted by Gitlin and Lyons (2008), these are the main building blocks of a proposal. It is usually best to outline the overall aim of the project, and then expand this into a number of specific objectives. The aims and objectives need to describe the research question or questions that will be addressed, and what the outcomes will be. They must be realistic and achievable. They must also be written clearly and concisely, in such a way that it will be possible to evaluate, once a project has been completed, whether or not they have been met (in other words, they must be specific and measurable). If the project involves an experimental approach you will need to include the specific hypotheses that will be tested. It is important that, when taken together, the objectives enable the overall aim or aims of the project to be met. To aid the reader, it is often useful to list objectives as a set of bullet points, starting each objective with the word 'to . . .'. Some examples of appropriately worded objectives are shown in Box 7.3. You should also remember to ensure that the objectives map on to the overall objectives of the funding organization. This may well involve including one or more objectives that set out how the proposed research would inform policy or practice, and contribute to quality of life, economic competitiveness, and so on.

Box 7.3 Examples of clearly worded objectives

- To provide a new body of data which will address hitherto neglected differences between experimental findings in the implicit memory and mere exposure literatures, and thus contribute to current knowledge and understanding of the two areas
- To suggest ways in which local authorities can improve the efficiency and speed of processing of applications for new residential dwellings, without compromising environmental concerns, nor the role of public consultation
- To design and implement a novel 3-D representation of sub-grid cloud structure
- To locate and identify plant pathogenic bacteria that confer either survival within, or killing of, host insects, in order to understand how pathogenic bacteria survive insect ingestion
- To generate new empirical data on the functioning of different types of partnerships in the Protestant Church aid chain
- To develop and test a new rehabilitative technique that could substantially improve the quality of life of Parkinson's Disease patients

---

- To determine the effects of provonal supplementation on neural activity and cognition in older adults, using a randomized, cross-over intervention trial
- To develop and compare three different classes of geometrical and statistical models of 3D image structures
- To develop practical procedures for assessing the cost-effectiveness and cost utility of recent policy interventions, which take into account the agents' adaptive behaviours
- To assess stakeholder acceptance of alternative forms of direct and indirect dietary interventions, and how these vary by regional location and socio-demographic factors
- To investigate the development of visual search abilities in young infants with Williams Syndrome, in comparison with unaffected infants

In the case of larger projects, such as EU projects that relate to specific calls for proposals, you may need to include a statement that shows how the objectives relate to the specific Framework call, and how the proposed research would contribute to the knowledge base and objectives of other relevant EU programmes, strategies, Green papers, or technology platforms. It might also be appropriate to comment on how the proposed project will draw on expertise and results of other relevant EU projects.

Background

For most proposals it will be important to show that your proposed research, and the specific aims and objectives, are supported by a theoretical framework. This may not be necessary in the case of very applied projects aimed at particular funding organizations, but most of the major funders will want to see the theoretical justification for, and context of, what you are proposing. This section should concisely summarize the previous work in the field that is specifically relevant to your proposal. You should cover only the most pertinent studies, ensuring that you include those which have been published most recently. This needs to be done in a thoughtful and integrated way. The literature review should lay the ground, including the theoretical foundation, for your proposed research and identify important gaps in knowledge which you intend to address. It should be clear from this section why your research is timely, innovative and important, and why the methods you choose to use are appropriate. It should persuade reviewers and assessors that you have a solid grasp of the subject matter. The section should include a description of any preliminary or pilot work that you have conducted that will help to convince assessors of the feasibility of what you want to do. This will help you to persuade assessors that you have the capability to complete the project. It is important to explain the relationship between the earlier work and the proposed project. At the end of this section it is important to include a summary sentence or two which make it explicit exactly how your specific project follows on from what has gone before and why it is important that it is carried out now.

Gitlin and Lyons (2008) list seven questions that you should ask yourself about your literature review:

- Does the review present important background information about the proposed topic?
- Does the literature review critically evaluate and synthesize existing knowledge?
- Are the identified gaps in knowledge addressed by the study?
- Does the review provide the basis of support for the hypotheses/research question?
- Has the need for the study been documented?
- Does the literature review appear complete and up to date?
- Is the review logically and systematically developed and presented?

(Gitlin and Lyons 2008: 84)

Methodology

This section addresses the important question of how you will carry out the proposed research, the methodology you will use and why it is appropriate. The choice of methodology should follow from the stated aims and objectives of the project. Your description of the methodology will vary depending on the type of methodology being used but, in each case, you will need to reassure assessors about the appropriateness and feasibility of your chosen methods. In the case of experimental studies, you will need to outline the specific research design or designs that you will use to test your hypotheses, the specific methods to be used and how you will collect, store and analyse the data. As far as specific methods and procedures are concerned, you will need to describe how you will do such things as extract samples of biological materials, treat specific cultures or samples, or create new gene libraries. For other types of research, you may need to describe how you will assess the functionality of a particular interface design or develop questionnaires and interview protocols, or run focus group sessions. You may need to describe how you will develop and test models or simulations, or analyse pieces of text, or use secondary data sources. In all cases, you will need to demonstrate a clear and systematic approach to the analysis of data, and show how it fits into the research design.

If you are testing or assessing human participants you will need to provide detail about your sampling strategy and recruitment procedures, including the inclusion and exclusion criteria you will use. It will need to be clear how many participants you plan to recruit, and whether this number is sufficient to enable you to reach sound conclusions (i.e. that the study will have sufficient power to test your hypotheses). If you plan to carry out a longitudinal study that goes on over several years, you will need to reassure assessors that you have taken account of potential drop-out rates. You will then need to describe how you will allocate participants to experimental conditions, ensuring that you are not introducing any unintended confounds into your design. The section also needs to include details of the particular measures that you will use. It is preferable to use known tests or instruments, so that assessors will be aware of their validity and reliability. Where this is not possible, you will need to convince assessors that your intended measures will be reliable and valid. Whatever your precise methodology, you will need to show that you have anticipated potential difficulties and addressed how they should be handled.

In some cases, the word limit for this section (or the overall word limit on the case for support) will not allow for this amount of detailed information. In such cases, it may be possible to enclose a technical annex. If not, you should refer to previous published work of yours that has used a similar methodology (where more detail is provided).

Unless asked for in a separate section, this section should include an outline of the planned timescale for the project, setting out key milestones and making it clear what will be achieved at each stage. A simple example is shown in Table 7.1. The timeplan must be realistic. Investigators, particularly new ones, tend to under-estimate the amount of start-up time needed to get a project off the ground. You need to allow for some slippage time as difficulties are almost always encountered at some stage (see Chapter 10).

Table 7.1 Example of a work timetable for a single partner project

Stage	No. of months
Completion of all preparation and design work	3
Commencement of fieldwork or material/information/data collection phase of study	2
Completion of fieldwork or collection phase of study	27
Commencement of analysis phase of study	10
Completion of analysis phase	32
Commencement of writing up of the research	18
Completion of preparation of datasets for archiving	36
Completion of writing up	36

In the case of larger projects, such as EU projects, the methods section may actually be structured in terms of the work to be carried out under each of the different workpackages, and the timing of these. Clearly, before doing this, it will have been necessary to determine how the work programme should be divided into distinct 'packages'. In describing the different workpackages, it needs to be clear what the outputs will be and how these feed into other workpackages. There are usually specific workpackages that relate to aspects of the project such as dissemination and project management, in addition to those relating to information and data gathering, synthesis and analysis of information, and so on. Some example overview descriptions of workpackages are shown in Box 7.4. These will be supplemented with much more detailed descriptions (often in tabular form), showing who is leading and who is contributing to each package and the amount of time involved, as well as the overall objectives, summary of proposed work, planned deliverables and timing of these, for each workpackage.

Box 7.4 Example of some workpackage overview descriptions

Workpackage 1 (1–9 months) starts with a benchmarking analysis of current and recent past use of relevant dietary intervention policies, and analyses of their effectiveness across the EU. The team will look at the extent to which a consistent picture emerges across countries in terms of the success or failure of the application of the different policies. The workpackage will have three main outputs: a) identification of relevant policy interventions across the EU, b) an evaluation of their effectiveness in terms of success in application, and c) selection of a number of case studies for Workpackage 2.

Workpackage 4 (8–33 months) builds on the actions that will emerge from Workpackages 1, 2 and 3. The workpackage examines consumer acceptance of alternative intervention strategies in a cross-national survey, using a representative sampling design. The approach is based on similar work conducted in our previous EU funded Project (Dietwise). The survey will take place in four different EU countries, which vary in cultural and economic factors. The findings will shed light on the public acceptance (or otherwise) of alternative intervention strategies in the different countries.

Workpackage 8 (1–48 months) involves project management, and will ensure that the project runs smoothly and to time. At each of the six-monthly partner meetings, we will review progress to date and make decisions about the work planned for the remainder of the project. Liaison with, and reporting to, the Commission will be continued, as appropriate, throughout the project.

Ethical considerations

In many areas of research, researchers need to get approval from one or more Research Ethics Committees before their project can proceed. Even where this is not the case, there may well be ethical issues that you need to take into consideration. Most funding organizations ask applicants to comment on any such ethical considerations, and to provide evidence that they have applied for, or received, appropriate ethical approval where this is needed. It is worth bearing in mind that receiving approval from some ethics committees can be a lengthy process. You should not wait until you know whether or not your research has been funded before seeking such approval. This could seriously delay the start date of the planned project and may not be acceptable to the funding organization. The process of applying for ethical approval of research projects is covered in more detail in Chapter 8.

Management plan

In the case of relatively simple projects, you may not need to complete a separate section relating to project management, but for some sponsors, and for all larger (particularly team based) proposals, this is likely to be required. The section needs to set out the individual roles of the different partners in the project, and explain how the project will be managed (by whom and in what way). It also needs to outline the roles of key research and other staff, and describe proposed management meeting schedules, and how information will be disseminated and shared between different project partners and team members. The section should also provide information about the planned timescale for the project, setting out the key milestones (and who will be responsible for these), and what will be achieved at each stage. You may need to produce a Gant chart. Overall, your proposal needs to show that you understand the importance of meeting objectives, timetable and budget and that the research team has the necessary skills and competences to deliver it.

Justification of resources

Virtually all funding organizations expect researchers to justify the need for the resources for which they are requesting funding. The key thing here is, first, to make a short clear case why you need funding for all of the items that you have included in your budget (unless these are very minor). Thus, you need to state why you need a particular piece of equipment, or to employ a dedicated research assistant with a certain level of experience, or to partially fund a technician or secretary, or to travel overseas or attend a particular conference. Do not assume that this is obvious and is therefore not worth stating. Where relevant (e.g. for most applications submitted using the Full Economic Costing methodology) you will also need to justify any Principal Investigator time that is being claimed as a directly allocated cost (see Chapter 9). You need to be realistic in terms of what you are requesting. Do not try to include the costs of items that are not absolutely necessary for the success of the project, or simply inflate the costs of standard items. On the other hand you should not try to save money by underestimating and under-costing what you require. The key point to remember is that you need to show how your proposal represents value for money. Most funders are not looking to support the 'cheapest' proposals. Rather they will be concerned to support those which are believed to offer the best value for money. Some example cost justification statements are shown in Box 7.5. Further examples are provided in Appendix 9.

Box 7.5 Examples of statements relating to justification of resources

The major resources requested relate to staffing. We request funding for a full-time postdoctoral assistant for one year. The planned experimental schedule and sophistication of techniques necessitate a full-time, postdoctoral appointment.

Due to the nature of the work, consumable costs are relatively high, with ELISAs (30 plates at an average of £420) and specific antibodies for use in western immunoblotting, confocal microscopy, and FACS, jointly costed at £24000. An additional £4000 is requested to cover other laboratory and IT related consumables over the course of the project.

We request funding for travel to two relevant major conferences (IST 2008, Oregon; Nanoscience and Materials 2009, Tokyo), and for collaborative visits to the University of Montreal to facilitate our ongoing collaboration with our Canadian partners (full details given in budget section). This is essential for dissemination, networking, and training and career development of the two postdoctoral research fellows and PhD students who will be attached to the project.

Outcomes and dissemination

Most funding organizations also expect applicants to comment on their plans for disseminating the outcomes of the proposed work, and for engaging with potential users and beneficiaries during the course of the project, where this is relevant. Referees will normally be asked to comment on this aspect of the proposal, so you need to produce a full response. Wherever possible, your dissemination plans should take account of appropriate non-academic, in addition to academic, audiences. These may include industry, government offices, schools, medical charities and self-help organizations and the media. Dissemination may be in the form of reports, articles, presentations, workshops and other events. An example of an appropriately worded dissemination statement is shown in Box 7.6. Three further examples are provided in Appendix 10.

Box 7.6 Example of an appropriately worded dissemination statement

The results of the research project will be disseminated to the scientific community via conference presentations at national and international meetings and by publication in internationally regarded peer review journals (including high profile science journals, such as *Nature and Science*, and high impact specialist journals, such as *Nanoletters*). Potential commercial implications of the results will be explored in collaboration with our Canadian partners under the provision of an IP agreement negotiated between the institutions prior to the start of the project. The University of Berkshire IP department will ensure appropriate protection and exploitation of any intellectual property that might arise from the project. Findings from the project will also feed into the South East Universities ongoing public lecture programme, as well as being disseminated to interested members of the general public through local open meetings such as Café Scientifique (currently coordinated through our University's Communications Office).

Summary

You should try to make space at the end of your case for support for a succinct summary statement that crisply covers what you propose to do, why this is important, why the work should be carried out by you and conducted in your organization, and what the expected outcomes and benefits will be. It is important to end on an upbeat note, which conveys your enthusiasm for the proposed work – after all, if you do not seem enthusiastic why should they be? An appropriate example of a summary statement is shown in Appendix 11.

Bibliography

You need to provide a condensed listing of the references you have cited in the case for support. Referees will make judgements about your likely knowledge of the literature, theoretical grounding and current state of the art of your subject area, from the references you choose to cite.

Letters of support

If your research requires access to specific facilities, or specific patient or other participant populations, it is important to get a letter of support from someone who is in a position to approve such access. Similarly, it is good to get letters of support from potential collaborators, particularly if they come from non-academic organizations. In the latter case, a strong letter of support can convince assessors that the collaboration is genuine, and will explain what the collaborator will contribute and how they will benefit. In their funding guidelines, EPSRC suggests that a good letter of support from a non-academic partner will:

- confirm commitment to the proposed project;
- explain clearly the value, relevance and possible benefits of the work to the collaborative partner;
- give the nature and equivalent value of any in-kind contribution;
- describe the added value of any industry or other involvement.

Letters of support are sent, along with the original proposal, to referees, for taking into account when making their assessment.

Nominating referees

Some funding organizations allow you to nominate (usually two) referees who might be approached to comment on the proposal. You should select experts in the area of research in question, who you feel would be able to give a fair assessment of your work. You should not select people whom you have worked too closely with in the past, or who come from your own institution, as these will not be considered to be appropriately independent by the funding organization. Office staff will generally approach at least one of your suggested referees when selecting a wider set of reviewers. You should make sure that your nominated referees are aware that you have named them in your proposals; indeed, it is courteous to ask their permission to do this. It is better for them to tell you at the outset if they are not willing to do this, rather than declining when the funding organization approaches them (which could result in your having no nominated referees).

Presenting your case clearly and convincingly

Having an innovative idea, or set of ideas, is critical to the success of any grant proposal, but presenting your ideas well is just as important. As Gitlin and Lyons (2008: 81) note, 'writing your ideas in a concise, clear manner is one of the most important components of the process of grantsmanship. Proposal writing involves a style that is technical, crisp and to the point. It is not an occasion to use a more literary, flowery, or embellished approach to writing'. The best advice is to write in succinct plain English, avoiding the use of too much technical jargon or redundant information. Try to adopt a positive style. You should use short sentences and paragraphs, but do not try to cut corners by using lots of abbreviations.

Your proposal needs to look good. You should avoid long pieces of dense text. Make sure there is plenty of white space, with line spaces between paragraphs. Use bullet points where appropriate. You should have clearly delineated sub-sections with sub-headings. The typeface and size should be selected for easy reading – some funders place restrictions on minimum size of typeface that can be used, and also on the minimum margin size. Finally you should always check the spelling and grammar, as an application that is full of spelling and simple grammatical errors will irritate assessors and referees.

Deciding when it's ready to submit

A former colleague, who was a member of a Research Council Grants Board, once started a presentation by stating that 'the number one characteristic of a successful grant application is that it is submitted'[1]. This may seem obvious, but unless you actually submit a proposal you will not stand any chance of success. Some researchers strive to produce the perfect proposal to such an extent that they are never satisfied with their application and never actually get to the point of submission. On the other hand, many researchers have a tendency to rush proposals and not appreciate the amount of time it takes to develop one that has a good chance of success. This characteristic is particularly associated with those at the start of their career who are anxious to get their work funded. Submitting a rushed, premature application, however, is nearly always a waste of time, effort and emotional energy. You must allow time for getting comments from relevant colleagues and for taking these on board. You should expect to make several iterations of your application before it is finally ready to go. As Gitlin and Lyons (2008: 118) note, 'you need to be prepared to write, re-write, and then write again'. If there is not time for this, it is usually better not to apply. Many of the major funding organizations (including all of the UK Research Councils) now routinely publish institutional (and sometimes department) success rates. Institutions will not look kindly on researchers who bring these rates down by submitting consistently low quality applications. Some funding organizations have adopted even stricter measures. As noted above, since spring 2009 EPSRC will only accept one application (in a one-year period) from applicants who have a particularly low success rate in the preceding years. Finally, it is important that you select a realistic start date for the proposed project. You should check with your institution's research support office, or consult the funding organization, about how long the assessment process is likely to take. For most major funders, however, a start date around six to nine months after the time of submission should be feasible.

Submitting your proposal

Most of the major funding organizations now insist on electronic submission of application forms. The UK Research Councils (with the exception of MRC) operate a standard Joint Electronic Submission (Je-S) System to handle all applications, reviewers' comments, and final grant reports. MRC currently operates its own Electronic Applications and Assessment (EAA) System. You will need the help of your institution's research support office to have access to, and use, these systems. You need to remember that the vast majority of funding organizations require that an official signatory of your institution reviews the budget and other details and confirms the accuracy of the information. Although the grant is awarded to an individual or research team, it is the institution that must assume legal responsibility for the conduct of the project and expenditure of funds. Your research support office will require a certain amount of time to check and sign off a grant proposal (usually between five and ten days) and you must allow for this in your planning.

When your proposal is received by the funding organization it will usually be checked by the office staff to ensure that you are eligible to apply for the scheme in question, and that you have completed the form correctly, conforming to the guidelines, and have included all the necessary information. If not, they will 'reject' the application at this stage. Applications may also be rejected at this stage if they are a resubmission of an earlier proposal, that has not been specifically invited and has not undergone sufficient revision. Provided the application passes this initial scrutiny, it will be forwarded to referees or assessors depending on the nature of the specific funding scheme.

Responding to reviewers

Many funding organizations allow applicants to respond to reviewers' comments before the proposal goes before the grants committee. The timescale will usually be fairly short, with applicants often having to make their response within a week. The response will then go to the assessment committee along with reviewers' comments.

If you are offered the opportunity to respond to reviewers' comments, then you should produce a response. What you say in this 'right to reply' is, in some ways, just as important as what you say in the original application, and can be critical to the success or failure of the application. The most important thing is for you to get the tone of your response correct. It is inevitably difficult to read reviewers' negative comments with any equanimity. Emotional detachment is virtually impossible to achieve. However, no matter how irritated you are by particular comments, your response should be calm and measured. You should not make discourteous or disparaging comments about the referees, or produce an arrogant or indignant response. If you feel that a referee has misunderstood something, do not provide a response that implies that the referee is stupid. Rather, you should acknowledge that the original application may not have been worded sufficiently clearly and take the opportunity to re-state the original point. A courteous, well constructed, robust and honest reply can be a persuasive part of the final decision-making process. It is an opportunity to clarify any misunderstandings that referees may have had, and to correct any factual errors in their comments. It is also an opportunity for you to display a level of planning and forethought beyond that which could be contained in the original project description. You can also include extra references to publications if you feel this helps you to answer the referees' points more convincingly.

Although most funders place an upper limit on the length of such responses, the allowance is often actually quite generous (given the restriction on the length of the original proposal). You should take the opportunity to use this allowance to address the comments fully, even ones that appear to be mildly positive. Referees have a habit of 'damning with faint praise'. For example, you might receive a comment such as

'The research could be of some benefit for the development of rehabilitation techniques for Parkinson's Disease patients.'

If you receive this type of statement, do not just thank the referee for the positive comment, or simply not respond at all (as it is not perceived to be a criticism). Rather you should say something like,

'We thank Referee A for the positive comment about the perceived benefit of our work for PD patients, but feel that he or she may have underestimated the full importance and significance of the work. Our findings should lead to the development of novel rehabilitation techniques that should considerably improve the quality of life of PD patients, and result in substantial cost savings for the NHS.'

Similarly, if a referee makes a comment such as

'The applicant appears to be sufficiently competent to carry out the proposed work'

a suitable response might be

'It may not be sufficiently clear from my CV, but I have successfully managed three previous externally funded research projects in this and similar areas. These projects have resulted in a total of 16 papers in international refereed journals. I am fully experienced at using the proposed methodological techniques and procedures, and working with the proposed patient population.'

It is usually best to structure your response with clear sub-headings, which could be the queries raised by each referee. You should then address each point succinctly and clearly. Some suggested examples of how to structure responses to specific issues raised by referees are shown in Appendix 12.

Finally, it is just as important to get feedback and advice from colleagues on your draft response, as on the original proposal. This may be a challenge given the length of time available, but it is worth doing. Interestingly, many applicants tend to feel that reading referees' comments and replying to them is a very private process. Nevertheless, it is much better to share comments with relevant colleagues (they will have undoubtedly received similar sorts of criticisms of their own proposals in the past) and get their advice on how best to respond. It is also worth getting advice from staff in your institution's research support office, as they are likely to have seen examples of responses associated with both successful and unsuccessful proposals.

Preparing for interviews

Some funding schemes have a two-stage process in which, following a short listing stage, selected applicants are invited for interview. This procedure tends to apply in competitions that are making major funding awards (such as EPSRC's Challenging Engineering Scheme) and in many of the schemes for funding personal fellowships. The interviewers on such occasions tend to be a sub-set of the relevant funding committee, including the Chair or Deputy Chair. The majority will not have detailed subject-specific knowledge of the area of research in which the applicant is proposing to work. The interview panel's questions will be based around the assessment criteria for the particular competition in question, and will pick up on issues that have been raised by the referees. In the case of fellowships, the panel will want to reassure themselves that the applicant has the ability and potential to benefit from the award and deliver the proposed research. The best way to prepare for such interviews is to arrange for a mock interview to be held within your institution. The mock interview should be run in a formal way (as the real process would) and should involve interviewers who resemble the types of people on the actual panel (i.e. senior staff from departments other than that of the applicant/s). Interviewers need to familiarize themselves with the proposal, the details of the scheme in question, the assessment criteria and the referees' comments if available. Before holding any mock interview, it is worth talking to an appropriate person in the funding organization to get their advice on the likely format of the interview and the topics that will be covered. Also remember that when it comes to the real interview, even though you may be feeling nervous, it is important to show enthusiasm for your proposed work. After all, if you are not enthusiastic, why should they be?

Coping with rejection

Whether a decision has been made on the basis of just a written application or an interview, many applicants receive a letter of rejection at the end of the process. We have seen in Chapter 3 that the success rates in many funding competitions are only modest, and that the majority of applicants are not successful. Receiving a letter of rejection can be enormously discouraging, particularly the first time it happens. Many applicants feel angry that they have been unfairly assessed in some way. Others simply feel frustrated and not clear how to move forward. The best advice is to read the letter, and feedback that is given, and then do nothing for a day or two. You should remember that negative comments will have their biggest impact on you the first time they are read. Coming back to them on a subsequent occasion will allow you to take a more measured view. By this time you should have got over the initial disappointment and will be thinking more rationally. You should not regard lack of success as a personal failure. When a grant application does not succeed, this may simply reflect the level of competition rather than any major weakness in the proposal. If you have not received any feedback at the rejection stage, you should ask the funding organization if any such feedback is available. Research Council office staff will usually provide some comments based on what was said at the grants board meeting, and the same thing often applies with other funding organizations. You need to reflect on this feedback and discuss it with others. You need to identify what you can learn from the feedback in terms of reshaping the proposal or moving your ideas forward in a different direction.

Some organizations will allow invited applicants to resubmit their proposals to take account of reviewers' and assessors' comments, although this is getting increasingly less common. In April 2009, for example, EPSRC announced that, in order to reduce pressure on the peer review system, they would no longer accept uninvited resubmissions of proposals. If you have not been invited to make a resubmission then it will not usually be possible to resubmit your proposal to the same funding organization (or to another Research Council in the case of Research Council applications), unless a major revision to the programme of work has been made. However, you may well be able to resubmit your proposal to a different organization (e.g. a research charity), but you should only do this if you are convinced that the proposal will stand a good chance of success (i.e. that it was rated highly by the original funding organization but that it did not quite make the funding cut-off point due to the high level of strong competition). If you decide to resubmit your work to a different funding organization, it is worth revising the proposal to take account of reviewers' and assessors' comments, where you feel this would strengthen the proposal, rather than simply submitting the original application.

Coping with success

Of course, the ideal outcome is to receive news from the funding body that your proposal has been successful. Although this is undoubtedly good news, the award of a grant does bring with it certain commitments and obligations. Chapter 10 looks at these in more detail.

Note

1   Professor Michael Breheny sadly died in 2002.

8

Ensuring ethical standards and applying for ethical approval

Informed consent • Responsibilities of host institutions • Research Ethics Committees • The application process • Ethical approval from the NHS

In many areas, it is now generally accepted that research studies must be designed and carried out in such a way as to conform to agreed ethical standards and principles. This applies whether you are working in the social, natural, physical, biological or medical sciences. Although there are some areas of research where ethical issues are not at stake, the importance of ethics in relation to research in many areas is so critical that it is appropriate to focus on this in the present chapter.

Three of the core ethical principles that apply to research are:

- avoidance of harm;
- respecting participants' rights and autonomy, for example by providing sufficient information to allow informed decision making;
- respecting confidentiality.

Thus, any research study you want to conduct must be designed in such a way as to avoid knowingly causing harm to participants or others affected by the research, and you must never try to coerce prospective participants into taking part in studies. Any financial recompense should be appropriate for the demands of the study and should not be so high as to act as an inducement to participate. Potential participants must be given full information about the purpose of the study and what will be required of them, and must sign a consent form to agree to take part. They must know that they are free to withdraw at any stage and that this will not have any negative consequences for them (e.g. in relation to subsequent care if they are a patient). The confidentiality of participants must also be respected at all times and any data or other material must be appropriately stored, in line with the requirements of the Data Protection Act. Wherever possible, you should also be 'honest' with those taking part, and not knowingly deceive them. In some cases, however, some minimal level of deception is acceptable if it is necessary for the design of your study and entails no foreseeable risk to participants. As an experimenter, you might not want to alert participants to the real purpose of your study in some cases as this would bias their performance. This might apply in tests of unintentional memory, for example, where the aim is to assess how much people remember about materials that they are not deliberately trying to memorize. However, if such deception is involved, you must fully debrief participants as to the true purpose of the study at the end of the session.

Many of the now commonly agreed ethical standards and principles stem from the Declaration of Helsinki, which was originally published in 1975 (World Medical Association 1975), and is still considered to be the leading authority or cornerstone of human research ethics. The Declaration was put in place as a result of concerns over participants being systematically abused in research studies. The most well cited examples of this were carried out in the Second World War concentration camps, but there have been more recent (although less severe) examples. Beecher (1966), for example, reported that 22 of the 50 studies that he reviewed were actually unethical in some way. The Declaration of Helsinki has been revised and updated several times over the years, with the sixth version being published in 2008 (World Medical Association 2008). The Declaration makes the point that research must conform to generally accepted scientific principles and be based on a thorough knowledge of the scientific literature. It requires that each potential participant be adequately informed about the aims, methods and anticipated benefits and potential risks of the study and any discomfort it might entail. The Declaration states that research involving human participants should only be conducted if the importance of the objectives outweighs the inherent risks and burdens.

Informed consent

A key consideration in relation to research ethics is the notion of informed consent. This is essential so that research participants understand the purpose of the proposed study and what will be required of them. In all areas of research with human participants, the key elements of informed consent are that

- participants understand the purpose and duration of research and procedures to be done;
- all reasonable foreseeable risks are explained;
- all reasonable benefits are explained;
- all appropriate alternatives to participation are disclosed;
- measures taken to protect confidentiality are described;
- participants understand that participation is voluntary and they can withdraw at any time with no detrimental consequences for them.

In general, you must provide participants with sufficient information in order to enable them to make an informed decision. It is not necessary to tell them every single detail about the study, as this might be overwhelming for them. You must achieve an appropriate balance between providing sufficient, but not unnecessary, information. Interestingly, for medical research studies, many countries require a higher level of disclosure of information for participation in research studies than for treatment.

Informed consent is based on the premise that the people giving consent are free from undue influence and that they have the capacity to provide consent. They must be able to understand the information that is presented to them, be able to weigh up the risks and benefits of taking part in the study, and actually believe that the information they are being given is truthful. However, some research may require the involvement of classes of people who are vulnerable in some way and/or unable to give consent. This includes children under the age of 16 and adults with cognitive or psychological impairment. In the case of research with children, consent must be obtained from parents or guardians when the children are under 16. Research Ethics Committees will look particularly hard at research proposals that involve the use of vulnerable populations, so you need to ensure that you anticipate their likely concerns.

It is now accepted practice that researchers will provide participants with an information sheet outlining the purpose of the study, what will be required of them, and any risks involved, as well as a consent form, which must be signed by the participant to confirm their willingness to take part in the study. Further information on these aspects is given later in the chapter.

Responsibilities of host institutions

Most funding organizations and institutions will require that the research they support is designed and conducted in such a way that it meets relevant ethical standards and principles, and that the researcher and host institution are committed to safeguarding good research conduct. All organizations in receipt of Research Council funding, for example, are required to have procedures in place to ensure that they comply with the RCUK Policy and Code of Conduct on the Governance of Good Research Conduct that was published in July 2009 (RCUK 2009). The Code stipulates that organizations in receipt of RCUK funding for research are obliged to have in place the following:

- Clear policy statements that include guidance on what is and what is not acceptable. These must be drawn to the attention of all new relevant staff on appointment and be easily accessible at all times (e.g. on websites and in manuals).
- Clear managerial arrangements, including published procedures for normal supervision and management of research conduct, integrity and ethical issues and for reporting by individuals of any concerns about poor practice. Procedures must clearly identify the senior person within the organization who is responsible for ensuring good research conduct.
- Training and mentoring policies and procedures that all relevant staff are aware of.
- Ethical application procedures, including procedures for obtaining fully informed consent.

The UK Research Integrity Office has also updated its Code of Practice for Research (UKRIO 2009), which includes a helpful checklist for researchers on key points of good practice in research projects that is applicable to all subject areas.

A number of the Research Councils, as well as other large funding organizations, have also put in place their own frameworks and guidelines for ensuring appropriate ethical standards of research. ESRC, for example, introduced a Research Ethics Framework for social science research in 1996, with the dignity, rights and welfare of research participants as the core criteria. Since that date, the council has only funded research where consideration has been given to the ethical principles set out in the framework. The framework is based around the following six key principles:

- Research should be designed, reviewed and undertaken to ensure integrity and quality.
- Research staff and students must be informed fully about the purpose, methods and intended possible uses of the research, what their participation in the research entails and what risks, if any, are involved.
- The confidentiality of information supplied by research subjects and the anonymity of respondents must be respected.
- Research participants must participate in a voluntary way, free from any coercion.
- Harm to research participants must be avoided.
- The independence of research must be clear, and any conflicts of interest or impartiality must be explicit.

Some funding organizations will insist on researchers already having 'ethical approval' for the proposed research at the time of application, whereas others do not. Instead, they require applicants to consider and comment on whether ethical approval will be required, and the form that such approval will take. Formal ethical approval is usually required for research that:

- involves vulnerable groups, such as children, young people, those with a learning disability or cognitive impairment, or individuals in a dependent or unequal relationship;
- involves groups where permission of a 'gatekeeper' is normally required for initial access to members, such as ethnic or cultural groups, or indigenous communities;
- involves sensitive topics, such as ethnic status, gender, mental health, sexual behaviour, illegal or political behaviour, or involves experience of violence, abuse or exploitation;
- involves deception or which is conducted without participants' full and informed consent at the time the study is carried out;
- involves access to records of personal or confidential information, including genetic or other biological information concerning identifiable individuals;
- would induce psychological stress, anxiety or humiliation or cause more than minimal pain;
- involves intrusive interventions and tests that would not normally be encountered in the course of everyday life, such as the administration of drugs or other substances, taking of tissue samples, the use of vigorous physical exercise, or techniques such as hydrotherapy and MRI scanning.

In addition, some funding organizations might have further guidelines and policies relating specifically to the use of animals in research or the use of human tissue, or taking of blood samples. As far as the latter is concerned, it is important for researchers in the UK to be aware of the provisions of the Human Tissue Act (Human Tissue Authority 2004), which regulates the consents required for the use or storage of 'material which consists of, or includes, human cells', and requires that anyone storing such material for research must have a licence from the Human Tissue Authority.

As noted at the outset, ethical issues arise in relation to a wide range of disciplines, including many outside the medical and natural sciences. In some of these disciplines, such as those in the social sciences, questions are increasingly being asked about whether following 'set ethical procedures' is sufficient, as opposed to researchers being ethically aware or having what is sometimes called 'ethical mindfulness'. Such matters are actively addressed within professional societies such as the British Psychological Society (BPS), British Sociological Association (BSA) and British Educational Research Association (BERA). Each of these organizations has published their own research ethics frameworks or statements. The BSA statement, for example, states that the purpose of the statement is to make members aware of ethical issues that may arise throughout the research process and to encourage members to take responsibility for their own ethical practice. The statement does not therefore provide a set of 'recipes' for resolving ethical choices or dilemmas. Although the BPS, BSA and BERA guidelines cover many of the key ethical issues that arise in relation to the medical and natural sciences (such as gaining fully informed consent and maintaining confidentiality), they also consider issues that are more likely to arise in relation to social science research (such as covert research, the use of performance incentives, and the use of deception). As far as deception is concerned, some critics have argued that studies that rely on deception should be avoided as such research causes the public to regard social scientists as manipulative and exploitative (e.g. Ortmann and Hertwig 1997). Others argue, however, that considerable useful and valid knowledge might never be accumulated if participants had foreknowledge of the complete purpose of study procedures. Accordingly, most professional society ethical frameworks and guidelines allow limited use of deception in research.

Before moving on to discuss the mechanics of applying for ethical approval of research, it is worth noting that there are additional ethical considerations that apply in relation to research that are typically not covered by Research Ethics Committees. One key area relates to publication and the assignment of authorship and to protecting the rights of those who have contributed to the research process, either by including them as joint authors or acknowledging their contribution in an appropriate way. Pressures on careers mean that disputes over assignment of publication credit are becoming increasingly common. Sandler and Russell (2005), for example, carried out a large survey and reported that over a quarter of respondents claimed to have fallen victim to unfair or unethical authorship assignments. This matter is returned to in Chapter 10.

Research Ethics Committees

At one time, research involving human participants was largely unregulated, but this is no longer the case. In 2001 the UK Department of Health, for example, published a Research Governance Framework for health and social care, which requires all health and social care research to be independently reviewed by ethics committees to ensure that it meets ethical standards. Similarly, in 1974, the US Department of Health and Human Services and Federal Drugs Administration (FDA) introduced regulations to protect human participants in research studies, which led to the establishment of Institutional Review Boards (the US equivalent of our Research Ethics Committees).

There are a number of different types of ethics committee. Some are run by individual academic institutions or research organizations, whereas others are run on a wider scale, with the most prominent in the UK being the NHS committees. Rather than being based in a single NHS Trust, the NHS Committees operate on a larger regional basis. If your proposed research is likely to require consideration by an REC, it is necessary to establish which committee or committees it should be reviewed by. Most academic institutions have formal RECs that help to ensure that the research conducted within the institution is conducted according to appropriate ethical standards. Such committees will also be responsible for reviewing applications for ethical approval of research. In some instances, certain types of research may have to be approved by more than one REC. The most typical examples of this are collaborative research projects that involve a number of different host institutions, and research that in some way involves the NHS (see below). Gaining approval from multiple RECs can be a frustrating process as most will have different forms requiring information to be presented in different ways, and the different committees may well raise different queries and issues that they want applicants to address.

Universities and other research organizations are responsible for ensuring that the RECs act independently. They must be free from bias and undue influence from the institution in which they are located, from the researchers whose proposals they consider, and from the personal or financial interests of their members. Institutions should therefore ensure that RECs include members who are independent of the institution, and should set out procedures for identifying and dealing with potential conflicts of interest. The membership of an REC is fundamental to ensuring that it has the appropriate range of expertise and the breadth of experience necessary to provide competent and rigorous review of the proposals submitted to it. ESRC recommends that institutional RECs are multidisciplinary, are comprised of both men and women and include at least one lay member from the local community. Members should have broad experience of and expertise in the areas of research regularly reviewed by the committee, and should have the confidence of the research community.

RECs should review research proposals in a way that is independent, competent and timely. Their primary role is to protect the dignity, rights and welfare of research participants. They should also have due regard to the consequences of the proposed research for others directly affected by it and to the interests of those who do not take part in the research but might benefit or suffer from its outcomes in the future, as well as the safety of the researchers themselves. RECs will consider each research proposal submitted and may either approve it as submitted, approve it subject to meeting specified conditions, or reject it on ethical grounds. The decision made for each proposal, and the grounds on which it was made, should be recorded and provided to the researchers, with a copy kept on file.

Some RECs may delegate responsibility for approving proposals to lower level sub-committees or to nominated individuals, where the research concerned is routine and not deemed to require judgement of the full committee. This might include research that does not involve patients or clients of health or social services, vulnerable groups or those not able to give consent, or deception, or procedures that might distress participants or involve an element of risk. In such cases, the sub-committee, or nominated individual, must ensure that the research will be conducted to a sufficiently high standard and in line with agreed ethical standards, and that fully informed consent is obtained from all participants.

As a researcher, you need to know which Ethics Committee or Committees will have to consider and approve your proposal in order for your research to go ahead, and what their procedures for assessing proposals entail.

The application process

Details of the application process will vary depending on the working practices of the specific REC that will consider the application. You will need to check on the procedures that will apply to your application, including the specification information that needs to be provided on the application form and in supporting documentation.

Application forms and protocols

Research proposals submitted for application to an REC might normally be expected to include the following information, although there will be some variation across individual RECs.

- aims of the research;
- scientific background of the research;
- study design;
- details of participants and recruitment process;
- methods of data collection and analysis;
- principal investigator's summary of potential ethical issues and how they will be addressed;
- benefits and risks to participants or third parties;
- risks to researchers;
- procedures for informed consent, including copies of the information sheet and consent form;
- expected outcomes and benefits of the research;
- how the results will be disseminated (including to participants);
- measures taken to ensure confidentiality, privacy and data protection.

Information sheets and consent forms

In general, any information sheet you give to participants must be on headed notepaper and include a contact name and telephone number of the lead investigator. The information sheet must be written in a language that can be easily understood by participants. It must include a summary of the research and its purposes, together with a clear account of what will be required of the participants. The following specific points will need to be covered:

• how participants are being selected;
• arrangements for informing each participant's GP, if appropriate;
• arrangements for expenses and other payments, if appropriate;
• arrangements to allow participants to withdraw at any stage if they wish;
• arrangements to ensure the confidentiality of any material collected during the project, and arrangements for its storage and eventual disposal;
• arrangements for publishing the research results and how confidentiality will be ensured;
• arrangements for providing participants with the results;
• a statement confirming that the research has received approval from an appropriate REC.

An example of an information sheet given to patients in a questionnaire study is shown in Appendix 13.

The consent form may be a separate document or may well be part of the same document as the information sheet. Participants will usually be required to sign the consent form in the presence of an independent witness (who also signs the form). The consent form, or consent section of the information sheet, will normally require participants to confirm that they have read and had explained to them the information sheet, and have had explained to them the purposes of the project and what will be required of them. They also have to confirm that their participation is voluntary and they have a right to withdraw from the project at any time (and, if relevant, without detriment to any care or services they will receive). Appendix 14 shows an example of a standard outline consent form that can be adapted to suit the purposes of specific studies.

The submission process

You will need to submit your application in line with the guidance to applicants provided by the relevant REC. The guidance notes should inform you of what will happen to your application once it has been submitted, and how long the review process should take. As noted above, decisions normally take one of three forms: approval, approval subject to the applicant addressing specific issues, or rejection. In many cases, applicants will be asked to provide further clarificatory information before a final decision is made. For example, they might be asked to reword specific questions that are used in interview protocols or on questionnaires. They may also be asked to address one or more questions, such as:

Do the research staff have the appropriate experience and expertise?

- If students are involved, is the research appropriate to be undertaken by students?
- Is there sufficient statistical power to the study?
- How will the investigators alleviate any concerns that might arise from reading the information sheet or from participation in the study?
- What will the investigators do if any participant's performance on any of the tests (e.g. of cognitive ability, or brain images) reveals any abnormalities?
- Will the research impact on the time of any staff employed by the organization where the study will be based?

It goes without saying that, as when responding to referees' comments, you should always ensure that your response to any requests for clarification or further information is courteous and appropriately worded, even if you feel that the committee is being unnecessarily cautious or 'picky'.

Subsequent amendments to your research

It is sometimes necessary to amend research protocols and planned procedures, after your application has been approved by an REC. For example, following pilot work on a healthy 'control' participant, you might decide that the intended procedure would be too time consuming for patients. You may therefore recommend shortening the procedure by reducing the number of study trials or sessions, or reducing the number of questions in a questionnaire. If you decide that you need to make any amendments, you will need to inform the relevant REC coordinator. If the amendments are significant then the revised protocol will normally need to go before the committee for re-approval.

Ethical approval from the NHS

Many research projects involve NHS patients or the use of NHS facilities. The NHS has developed a stringent system for establishing RECs and for reviewing proposals.

NHS Research Ethics Committees

The NHS runs a National Research Ethics Service (NRES) which oversees ethical matters in relation to NHS associated research. Within this, there are several different types of NHS REC within the UK that review different kinds of studies. These include local single RECs and multiple RECs. To find your local NHS REC there is a searchable directory of UK RECs, including their contact details and meeting dates, on the website of the National Research Ethics Service

Most committees meet monthly, and provide information on the dates by which applications have to be submitted in order to be considered at particular meetings. Decisions are normally made within 60 calendar days. The NRES supports an Integrated Research Application System (IRAS) that is a single system for applying for permission and approvals for health and social care research in the UK. It streamlines the process for seeking relevant approvals, as applicants do not need to submit multiple applications to more than one local NHS committee. Applications, for either single-site or multiple-site research, are submitted via a national electronic application system. Researchers for NHS associated research are also required to gain NHS R&D approval from the relevant local R&D office (e.g. that is based within the Healthcare Trust in which they want to conduct the research). There is now an integrated system for applying for both forms of approval, through the IRAS. Further details on the application process are given below.

In general, the following types of research must go to NHS Ethics Committees. Research that involves:

- patients and users of the NHS;
- carers and relatives of NHS patients;
- access to data, organs or other bodily material of past and present patients;
- fetal material and IVF involving NHS patients;
- the recently dead in NHS premises;
- use of NHS premises or facilities;
- NHS staff recruited by virtue of their professional role.

The NHS submission process

If you need to obtain NHS approval for your research project, you will need to submit your application on the standard form, available on the NRES website. It is important that you read the question-specific guidance notes before completing the form. Once you have completed your application form, you will need to 'book a slot' with an NHS REC. To do this you need to contact your local REC coordinator, if the research is based only in that one locality, or alternatively use the Central Allocation System. Bookings are normally made by telephone. You will be asked a number of questions, including the following:

- the name, title and contact details of the chief investigator;
- whether all the supporting documentation is complete;
- whether the application has been signed by the chief investigator;
- whether the study is a clinical trial of an investigational medicinal product or device;
- whether the research involves the use of radiation;
- whether it involves more than one domain or site and, if so, if it requires separate site-specific assessments;
- whether the research involves people unable to consent for themselves;

- whether funding has been secured;
- whether the application has previously been rejected by an REC;
- whether any of the named investigators are members of an NHS REC.

At the end of the process, you will be given a project reference number. You will then need to enter this into the electronic application form before completing the application. The NHS application form is fairly lengthy and is structured into a number of sub-sections which cover the following aspects: project title; details of investigators; proposed dates and duration of study; research objectives; scientific background and justification for research; summary of design and methodology, including details of any interventions or procedures; details of participants and how they will be recruited; procedures for seeking informed consent and the nature of any participant payments; how the data will be stored and confidentiality maintained; how the statistical aspects will be reviewed; how the results will be disseminated; and arrangements for monitoring the conduct of the research and any insurance arrangements.

Once you have completed your application form, you will need to lock the application (so that it cannot be changed) and print off a copy, as all signatures have to be completed in ink. You will then need to submit the application by post. Provided your application form has been completed correctly and has all the appropriate signatures, you will be sent a validation letter from the relevant REC coordinator. If the research involves one or more separate site-specific assessments, you will need to submit a site-specific form and CV of the lead investigator at that site, to the local REC coordinator for that site. This can only be done once you have received a validation letter from the primary REC. The site-specific form will require information about the arrangements for management and monitoring of the conduct of research on the site, and the name of the person with overall responsibility for this. It will also require details of any measures to minimize risks to participants on the site, and procedures and a contact point at the site for further information or clarification about the study or for making any complaints.

Review process

The relevant REC will consider the proposal at the designated meeting. As an applicant, you can normally attend the meeting if you wish to be present to address any points that committee members might raise. However, the committee will continue to discuss proposals once you or other investigators have been asked to leave, and will not make a decision in the presence of any investigators. Applicants are informed of the committee's decision in writing (within the specified time period). In some instances, the committee may seek further clarificatory information before making a decision, or suggest minor changes to the study procedures. For example, you might be required to produce separate information sheets for different phases of the study rather than having one combined information sheet, or to increase the length of time participants will be given to study the information sheet. Similarly, the committee might suggest that you use an alternative measure to the one proposed, and you are asked to comment on this suggestion and amend the protocol if you feel it is appropriate. If the committee does request any further information, the 60-day decision period will be suspended while the committee awaits a written response from the applicant. In the case of multi-site studies, each site-specific assessor will notify the main REC coordinator whether or not they have any objections. Requests for amendments to projects, once approval has been granted, need to be sent to the primary REC coordinator. As noted above, significant amendments will need to go back to the committee for approval.

NHS sponsors and R&D approval

Any research requiring collaboration of the NHS must have an individual or organization willing and able to take on the responsibilities of the research sponsor. The sponsor takes primary responsibility for ensuring that the design of the study meets appropriate standards and that arrangements are in place to ensure appropriate conduct and reporting. In addition to this, R&D management approval is required at each site before research can begin. An application for R&D management approval may be made alongside the application (using the IRAS). Ethics Committees will expect applicants to have held early discussions with relevant R&D offices. However, final R&D management approval will not be given until after a favourable ethical opinion has been given.

9

Costing a proposal

Determining what resources you need • Full economic costing • Costing versus pricing • Determining the full economic cost • Costing an fEC proposal (e.g. for a UK Research Council) • European Union projects • Pricing policies • Intellectual Property

A key part of applying for research funding is to determine what resources you will need to carry out the proposed project, and to price these appropriately. Within most institutions that are eligible to hold grants, there are fixed policies and guidelines for doing this. In developing your budget you will need to work with your institution's Research Development or Finance Office.

Determining what resources you need

Once you have a clear idea about your proposed programme of work, you need to think about what resources will be needed, in terms of such things as staffing, equipment, consumables, travel and other costs. It is very important that the specific resources you request are realistic and can be adequately justified. Trying to do things 'on the cheap' will be frowned upon by most funding organizations just as much as over-inflating your budget. If the estimation of resources needed, and the associated costings, are not realistic, research funders will have less confidence that you can carry out the proposed project appropriately.

Staffing costs make up the major part of the cost of many projects. You need to estimate how much staff time will be required to carry out the project, and what job categories and levels of experience will be needed. For many projects, you may simply need one full-time research assistant, either at postdoctoral or postgraduate level, depending on the degree of independence that they will have to show when carrying out the project. The proposed employment period will depend on the amount of work in the project plan. Sometimes the amount of work may require more than one researcher, possibly with different skills and levels of experience. If you do not have particular individuals in mind to fill the posts, salary levels are usually estimated below a fixed point on the appropriate salary scale. If you know who will be working on the project, and their salary would exceed this, you will usually need to make a special case to the funding organization in order to allow you to employ the person at a higher level; for example, by saying that the project requires their specific skills and experience level.

In addition to research staff, your project may also require dedicated technical or clerical staff input. Again, you need to estimate the time and level of experience that will be needed. Where the amount of time required does not amount to a full-time or, say, half-time position, many institutions allow grant-holders to 'buy out' time from their full-time permanent support staff. As noted in Chapter 7, you will need to discuss any such arrangements with your Head of Department before preparing a budget. The increased emphasis on collaborative projects and on the importance of making international linkages has encouraged some research funders to allow applicants to include requests for funding to bring overseas researchers to the UK to spend some time contributing to the proposed project. In larger collaborative projects, some funders will also allow applicants to request funding to cover the cost of project management and administration. Finally, since the implementation of full economic costing (fEC), many UK funders now allow applicants to include the cost of a proportion of their own time as part of the budget (see below). In such cases, you need to estimate the average number of hours per week that you will devote to the project, and then consult with staff in your institution's Research Development or Finance Office to determine the appropriate 'price per hour'.

You will also need to determine what equipment, consumables and other materials you will need to support the proposed research. When pricing these, you will have to refer to your institution's purchasing policy and guidelines. You should also check which items the funding organization will and will not allow you to include in your budgets. Many funders expect institutions to provide a certain level of equipment and other support, and will only provide funding for items, within a certain cost bracket, that are specifically needed for dedicated work on the project. If in doubt, staff in your Research Development Office should be able to advise you. In some cases, rather than purchasing equipment, you may need to request funding to buy time on national or international major research facilities, such as large lasers, synchrotrons, super computers, or telescopes. In some cases, this will need to be done directly, e.g. through the Science and Technology Facilities Research Council, whereas in other cases it will be indirectly through another funding organization, such as one of the UK Research Councils. In the latter case, you will need to complete a facility-relevant application form and submit this with your research proposal. If the funding organization decides to support the proposed research, you will need to confirm access arrangements with those responsible for allocating time on the facility.

For some experimental projects, you will need to claim funding to cover the cost of payments and expenses for human participants. To set the budget for this, you will need to estimate the number of participant hours needed for the proposed experiments. Other experimental projects may require the purchase and upkeep of animals. Most institutions will have fixed rates for this.

Finally, most applications include requests for funding for travel, either as a necessary part of the project (e.g. for meetings with other project partners, or travel to meet with participants or use special collections based elsewhere) or to scientific meetings and conferences where the results of the proposed research can be disseminated. In the latter case, you need to ensure that what you request is in line with the research funder's guidelines (for example, some only allow one international journey per applicant and researcher per year).

As outlined in Chapter 7, most funders require applicants to justify the types and levels of resource requested as part of the presentation of their cases for support. Box 7.5 (p. 102) and Appendix 9 show some examples of such justifications.

Full economic costing

As noted in Chapter 1, since 2006 the UK Research Councils only sponsor research on an fEC basis. What they mean by a 'full economic cost' is a price which, if recovered across an institution's full programme, would recover the total cost (direct, indirect and total overhead) of the research, including an adequate recurring investment in the institution's infrastructure. The Research Councils pay an agreed proportion of the fEC (currently 80 per cent) and institutions have to make up the shortfall. Other research funders pay different proportions of fEC, depending on their policies and procedures. UK charities, for example, pay zero per cent whereas government departments normally pay 100 per cent. Many industrial and commercial firms will also sponsor research on a 100 per cent fEC basis. Your university should have a pricing policy that will determine the level of fEC that needs to be charged (see below).

Costing versus pricing

Before getting into the details of full economic costing, it is worth making a distinction between the cost of research and the price that is charged. As might be obvious, the 'research cost' refers to the actual cost of carrying out the proposed research. To calculate this, it is necessary to include all less obvious, almost hidden, costs in addition to the more obvious direct costs (such as for staffing, equipment, and so on). Such hidden or less obvious costs include such things as contributions towards the cost of estates and support services. Your institution will have fixed rates that are charged for such things (see below).

In contrast to the cost, the price of a project is what the institution decides to charge the research funder for the proposed work. In some cases, the institution has no say in the matter. As noted above, for example, the UK Research Councils currently contribute 80 per cent towards the full economic cost, whereas most UK charities only fund direct project costs, with no additional 'overhead' charge. In other cases, it may be up to the institution to set the appropriate price. This usually applies to industrial and commercially funded research. Many institutions will have pricing policies to help researchers determine the appropriate price (see below). For example, it might be the policy to charge at least 100 per cent fEC for all commercially sponsored research, and to increase the price above this level for research where the academic benefit to the institution is less strong (for example, where the research funder insists on retaining the Intellectual Property Rights). Prices above 100 per cent may also be charged where the researcher and the institution are virtually 'uniquely positioned' to carry out the research and there is no effective competition. In some cases, there might be justification for charging a price that is below the 100 per cent fEC rate. This might be because it is strategically important to the organization to work with the sponsor or to carry out the proposed research. In all cases, however, institutions will have to calculate the full economic cost before determining the price.

In other cases, research funders may propose a fixed sum of money that they are willing to pay for the research, and it is up to the institution to set a budget that falls within this upper limit. The institution will have to decide whether it is feasible to undertake the proposed programme of work, based on a calculation of its full economic cost, for the amount of funding being offered. If not, they may decide to decline the project.

Determining the full economic cost

As outlined in Chapter 1, institutions use the Transparent Approach to Costing (TRAC) methodology (HEFCE 2005) to calculate the full economic costs of research. According to this methodology, costs are divided into the following four summary cost headings:

- directly incurred costs;
- directly allocated costs;
- indirect costs;
- exceptional items.

Each of these categories is described below.

Directly incurred costs

Directly incurred costs equate more or less to the direct costs of the project that have traditionally been included in budgets. These are costs that are charged to projects based on the amounts actually spent, and are fully auditable. Directly incurred costs usually fall into four sub-categories:

- *Staff* This includes researchers, clerical and any other staff who spend dedicated time on the project. Costs are based on the actual, as opposed to estimated, time spent. Any 'directly incurred' member of staff who spends less than 100 per cent of their time on the project will need to complete a project time record. You can only include technicians as a directly incurred cost item if they spend 100 per cent of their time dedicated to the project. If a lower proportion of their time is spent on the project then they fall under the directly allocated costs category.

  When calculating staff costs, for budget purposes, salary increments over the period of the project should be taken into account but not anticipated future pay awards (unless the funding organization specifically requires applicants to do this).
- *Equipment* The UK Research Councils define equipment as any single item of equipment over £3000. Research Councils will pay 80 per cent fEC for the first £50000 of total equipment costs and 100 per cent fEC for amounts above £50000 (but in the latter case this counts as an exceptional item – see below). Most of the major funding organizations require institutions to provide three quotations for items of equipment costing more than £25000.
- *Travel and subsistence* Travel costs for journeys that are an essential part of the investigation and are directly related to your research project can be claimed as a direct cost on the research grant. You must identify all journeys individually, and charges must be in line with your institution's own policies. Costs for attendance at scientific meetings and conferences may also be included where such attendance will be of direct benefit to your research (and its dissemination). Again, conferences need to be individually identified.
- *Other costs* This category includes all direct costs that are not included under

one of the above headings, such as equipment items costing less than £3000, consumables, software and software licences, publication costs, consultancy fees, recruitment and advertising, equipment maintenance charges and payments to experimental participants.

Directly allocated costs

Directly allocated costs are costs that are charged to projects on the basis of estimates, rather than direct costs. There are five sub-headings of directly allocated costs.

- Investigators. As a Principal or Co-investigator, you must estimate the number of hours you will spend on the project over the life of the project. This time period is then multiplied by the appropriate (institution determined) hourly rate. The UK Research Councils set a maximum total number of hours per year (across projects) that any one investigator can claim. Estimations of time need to cover all time spent on work relating to the project (once it has been awarded), including management and administration of the project, supervision of project staff, preparation of publications and presentations of findings. You cannot include time spent preparing the proposal. Some funding organizations require investigators to keep time sheets so that these charges can be verified if necessary.
- Technicians who spend less than 100 per cent of their time on the project. Again, time is allocated in a similar way to that of investigators.
- Charge out costs for use of major facilities or existing equipment, and other department services.
- Animal costs (if not claimed as directly incurred costs).
- Estates costs. These include a contribution towards the costs of buildings and utilities (e.g. electricity), as well as equipment maintenance and operational costs that have not been included under other cost headings. Estate costs are charged to projects using an agreed rate per person working on the project per annum. Most institutions have two estates rates – one for 'laboratory projects' and one for 'classroom based projects'.

Indirect costs

This category covers the costs of all central and department support services, such as personnel, finance, and library services. A single agreed rate is charged per person working on the project per annum.

Exceptions

Exceptions are specific categories of costs that the UK Research Councils have agreed they will fund in full at 100 per cent fEC. They include equipment costs above the £50 000 threshold for directly incurred costs, and any studentships that are directly associated with the project.

Table 9.1 shows a summary of which costs are normally included under each of the four headings.

Table 9.1 Breakdown of costs that are normally included under each of the four summary headings

Directly Incurred Costs	Directly Allocated Costs	Indirect Costs	Exceptions (UK Research Councils only)
Researchers	Investigators	At a £ per FTE per year for investigators and researchers	Total equipment over £50000
Technicians who spend 100% time on project	Technicians who spend less than 100% time on project	Covers central and department support services	Project studentships
Other staff e.g. clerical	Estate costs		
Travel and subsistence	Other directly allocated costs		
Consumables			
Equipment (between £3000 and £50000 in total)			
Other directly incurred costs			

Costing an fEC proposal (e.g. for a UK Research Council)

It is usually helpful to start by compiling a list of all of the resources you will need to request in order to carry out the proposed project. Most of these will come under the heading of 'directly incurred costs' but some (e.g. PI time) could be 'directly allocated costs'. Box 9.1 shows an example of such a list in relation to a hypothetical three-year BBSRC project grant.

Box 9.1 Summary list of resources that might be needed for a three-year BBSRC project

1 Researcher: Grade 6. Point 30. 100% fte. Start date – 1.10.2010 for 36 months
2 Technician: Grade 5. Point 25. 20% fte. Start date – 1.1.2011 for 24 months
3 Principal investigator time: 4 hours per week (for 36 months)
4 Co-investigator time: 2 hours per week (for 36 months)

---

5   Equipment: RMI PC £1855 (inc. VAT)
                 17" CRT monitor £180 (inc. VAT)
                 HP Colour printer £280 (inc. VAT)
6   Use of shared facilities. Dedicated time on BioAnalyser (40 runs @ £38 per run) = £1520
7   Other costs:
    a   Software licences £850
    b   Cell culture Plasticware £4000
    c   Cell culture Reagents £5200
    d   Other laboratory consumables £3000
8   Travel and subsistence
    a   Two persons (PI and RA) to attend national neurodegeneration conference, Cambridge UK, September 2011   £1400
    b   Two persons (PI and RA) to attend international neuroscience meeting, Oregon, US, September 2012   £3000

Once you have drawn up this list, you will need to get further information for many of the items in order to prepare the budget and calculate the total cost of the research. For example, in terms of research staff you would need to check the appropriate salary level (including National Insurance and pension costs) for the grade requested and make allowances for subsequent annual increments (unless the funder automatically commits to covering annual pay awards). Similarly, to calculate the total amount of funding needed to cover PI or Co-investigator time to be spent on the project you will need to calculate the number of hours that will be spent over the course of the project by multiplying the average estimated hours per week by the number of weeks worked per year (e.g. 44) by the number of years duration. The overall total number of hours then needs to be multiplied by the average estimated salary over the duration of the project (including National Insurance and pension contributions). Your university's research development or finance office will be able to assist you with these aspects.

To calculate costs of equipment, you will need to get current quotations from manufacturers, in line with your organization's purchasing policy. If you need to request funding to buy time on larger shared research facilities (either in your own organization or elsewhere) you will need to find out the relevant pricing structure (e.g. £x per hour or £y per run) and calculate the total number of hours or runs needed to carry out the proposed work. Some directly incurred costs for small, inexpensive items can be grouped together under a single heading, such as 'software licences' or 'other consumables' (e.g. cables, solder, dissection instruments, etc.), and an overall estimate included. Other costs, such as for attendance at national and international conferences, will have to be estimated as you will not know the exact amount of funding that will be required. It is important that these estimates are sufficiently informed so that they are sufficient to cover the costs of what will actually be required, but they are not excessive (and seen to be excessive). You need to remember that you (and your finance office) will have to account for the funding that is awarded and claimed, and have appropriate documentation in place.

Other directly allocated costs, such as estates costs and indirect costs are calculated on a formulaic basis, and your research development or finance office will have systems in place for doing this automatically.

Appendix 15 shows an example of how the relevant financial sections of a BBSRC application form might be completed in relation to the list of resources shown in Box 9.1 (p. 130).

European Union projects

Costing EU projects is complex and should be done in conjunction with an experienced person from your research development or finance office. For most EU projects (including Framework projects and ERC projects) the following guidelines apply.

- *Staff* Costs of all staff working on the project can be claimed (including centrally funded investigators). Costs should include incremental progression and allowance for future pay awards. All staff with time allocated to the project will need to complete time sheets, using an agreed template.
- *PhD students* Most EU projects allow you to claim the cost of PhD stipends for students working on the project. However, they do not allow you to claim for the cost of university fees.
- *Equipment* EU will only fund equipment that is essential for the project and wholly used on the project. They will not typically pay for desktop computers that might be used for a range of other purposes. VAT payments are not eligible costs and cannot be claimed back from Customs and Excise.
- *Travel* You can budget for costs associated with the project, but VAT and airport taxes are not eligible.
- *Consumables* These are eligible costs provided that they are only used on the project.
- *Audit costs* These need to be included for larger projects.
- *Exchange rates* When costing projects, it is sensible to use an exchange rate that is higher than the current rate. You should seek advice from your research development or finance office.
- *Indirect costs* For Framework projects, most universities currently use a transitional flat rate of 60 per cent of direct costs, but you need to consult with your research development or finance office for further advice on this. The situation is complicated by the fact that FP7 projects are made up of different activities which have different reimbursement rates. For ERC projects,

the indirect rate is 20 per cent of direct costs. The costs are not split into activities, however, and all costs are reimbursed at 100 per cent.

Pricing policies

As noted above, most institutions will have agreed pricing policies to guide researchers in determining the price of a project (based on the calculated full economic cost), where there is some flexibility. This normally applies to most industry and commercially sponsored research, as well as subcontract work with other universities. The price charged will depend on the extent to which the institution will benefit from carrying out the research, and how strategically important it is to establish or maintain a relationship with the research funder.

Where prices below 100 per cent fEC are charged, the institution will have to make up the difference from other funding, often from its QR income. The UK Government has set out a number of principles that need to be taken into consideration when determining whether institutions should use any of their public funding (such as QR) to support research that is not costed on a 100 per cent fEC basis. One such principle, for example, would be that the research should demonstrably contribute to the enhancement of the UK research base or in some other way provide a public scientific good. Thus, institutions need to ask themselves the following questions:

- Is the project intended to lead to new knowledge of a fundamental nature?
- Is the project likely to produce highly trained researchers for the enhancement of the research base or the wider benefit of the UK?
- Do the conditions of the award allow for the open publication of results without delay or approval by the sponsor?
- Do the conditions of the award allow institutions to retain benefits of the exploitation of any IP arising from the work (or share them with the charity in the case of charity funded research)?
- Does the sponsor use peer review, or an equivalent objective and robust process, to assess the quality of the research programme when determining whether or not to fund it?

Intellectual Property

Before finishing this chapter, it is worth saying a few words about IP given that consideration of this features in many institutional pricing policies. IP can be defined as a category of intangible rights protecting commercially valuable products of human intellect. Like other forms of property, it has an owner, can be bought or rented, and must be sufficiently protected. Most institutions have a Code of Practice to cover all forms of legally recognized IP that are created or devised in the course of employment of its staff. In addition, the UK Intellectual Property Office has produced comprehensive guidelines on what constitutes IP, and how to apply for Intellectual Property Rights. IP covers both copyright laws protecting creative works and industrial properties. If IP arises from research which is supported or commissioned by a third party (such as a Research Council, charity, industry, etc.), under a grant or contract, then the terms of the contractual agreement should determine ownership, use, commercial exploitation and rights of the institution. IP should not be given up lightly as it is often the only product that the university will have from carrying out the research. Hence, where IP is handed over to the research funder, institutions would normally expect to receive a higher than 100 fEC rate. Chapter 10 returns to the issue of IP rights when considering the commercial exploitation of funded research.

10

Gaining momentum

Negotiating contract details • Accepting the award and setting up a project account • Employing staff • Project management • Managing staff development • Leadership styles and skills • Research leadership on a wider front • Collaborating with others • Coping with difficulties • Building and sustaining a team • Shaping the funding agenda • Dissemination • Collaborating with industry • Commercial exploitation • Final words

The news that your proposal has been successful and is to be funded is undoubtedly good news. You will now have the resource to carry out the proposed research. However, the award of a grant also brings with it certain obligations and commitments: to the funding organization, to your institution, to project partners and to any staff whom you employ. This chapter takes you through some of the processes that you will have to go through, from negotiating contract details and setting up the initial project account, through employing and managing staff, to running a successful group funded by a range of sources, or leading research on a wider basis. It also looks at the need to diversify funding sources, including collaborating with industry, and commercially exploiting research outcomes.

Negotiating contract details

Many grant awards are very straightforward and you are awarded the funding that you have requested. In other cases, however, the funding organization may offer a reduced amount of funding and require you to revise your budget to take account of this. Occasionally, grants committees make an award on the basis that one line of work is taken out of the proposal. This requires the applicant to revise the work plan and budget to take account of this. You should involve your institution's Research Development or Finance Office in any such discussions and negotiations with funders. With some large multi-partner awards there is an automatic contract negotiation phase after projects have been provisionally approved. This applies to most European Union awards, for example. In this case, the contract negotiation phase can be quite lengthy as it involves several institutions. Again, it is important that this is done in full consultation with the experts in your Research Development Office.

Accepting the award and setting up a project account

In the case of the majority of funding organizations, grant awards are formally made to the institution rather than to the investigator or investigators concerned. It is therefore the duty of the institution formally to accept the award when they receive the offer letter. Once this has happened, the Research Accounts or Finance Department in your institution can set up a project account that you, as Principal Investigator (or lead investigator within your institution in the case of some joint projects), will have to manage. It is worth noting that it usually takes several weeks, after you hear that your application was successful, until you receive the formal offer letter. You need to allow for this in your planning and projected timescales. Your Research Accounts or Finance Office will normally set up a budget for your project that is based on the one included in the proposal. You will have responsibility for managing spending so that it is in line with this budget. With most funding organizations, grant holders have only a little leeway to vire spending from one category to another. Thus, if you applied for £98 000 for staffing costs, you cannot spend half of this on equipment (certainly not without the prior permission of the funding organization). However, there is normally some facility to allow you to vire a small proportion of the funding from one category to another. The conditions of award that accompany the offer letter should set this out. If in doubt, your Research Accounts or Finance Office will be able to advise you.

Most funding organizations will require annual (although sometimes more frequent) statements of expenditure. These will normally be produced by your Research Accounts or Finance Office. The Office will also need to complete and return an end of grant financial statement within three months of the end of the award. In addition, a few funders may require further administrative information to be provided, such as completion of monthly time sheets.

Finally, many funding organizations will require the award holder to produce an (academic) end of grant report, and (in the case of longer projects) some may require interim progress reports. Final reports must be submitted by the due date (in the case of the UK Research Councils, within three months from the end of grant), otherwise the funding organization may hold back the final financial payment. The purpose of the reports is to enable the funding organization to assess whether the work for which the grant was awarded has been carried out to an acceptable standard and whether value for money has been achieved. Grant holders will be required to report on matters such as main achievements in the light of the specific objectives that were set, publications and other outputs, other dissemination activities and knowledge transfer, and staff training and development.

Employing staff

Many funded projects will entail the need to employ staff. Sometimes you will know before an award is made who will be employed on the project, as their details were included in the application. In such cases, you will simply need to discuss with your Human Resources (HR) department how to set up contracts. Although it may not be formally necessary to produce formal job descriptions for such positions (as it is when employing new staff), it is nevertheless advisable to produce a job description that makes it clear what is expected of any staff you are employing. This can be referred to when reviewing project progress and staff development, and can be particularly useful in the case of any dispute.

Some research grant proposals also include funding for buying out part of the time of existing staff in the organization, most notably technical and clerical staff. In such cases, you need to negotiate with the Head of School or whoever is responsible for approving access to the time of such people.

In many cases, the award of a grant will require you to employ one or more new members of staff. You will have to ensure that the process for doing this is in line with your institution's employment policy and practices, in addition to national laws and regulations. In the UK, as in many other countries, employment practices must comply with Equal Opportunities legislation. The law requires that no job applicant or employee will receive less favourable treatment on the grounds of age, race, colour, nationality, ethnic or national origins, disability, gender, gender reassignment, marital status and trade union membership or in relation to a spent offence under the Rehabilitation of Offenders Act 1994.

Most universities insist that all posts for new staff are advertised (either internally and/or externally) and that objective criteria, in the form of job descriptions and person specifications, are developed for all posts. Shortlisting and interview procedures must include recording reasons for not selecting and appointing candidates. Your Human Resources department will be able to give you further detailed advice in relation to such matters. They will also be able to advise you on procedures for advertising posts. Most universities use the Jobs.ac.uk website (and their own internal website), either in addition to, or instead of, advertising in local and national newspapers, trade papers, magazines, etc. The latter can be fairly costly and you will need to check whether there is a budget for advertising. Some funders will allow you to cover this as part of your overall project budget but many will not.

As noted above, you will need to produce a job description and person specification for all new posts. The job description defines a post in relation to the responsibilities, tasks and duties the post holder is required to undertake. It also indicates the reporting relationships with the immediate line manager and any subordinates. The job description forms the basis for the person specification, which describes the knowledge, skills and attributes needed to perform the job. The person specification provides the basis for the selection process. An example job description and person specification for a research assistant post are shown in Box 10.1 and Table 10.1. You should note that when shortlisting and interviewing applicants, you need to establish a selection panel, rather than simply do this by yourself. You need to ensure that the membership of any panel is not gender biased; thus, if both male and female candidates are being interviewed, the panel must also include at least one male and one female member. Once you have selected the staff you want to employ, then your institution will need to draw up, and send them, a formal letter of employment and contract documents.

Box 10.1 Example job description for a postdoctoral research assistant

Post Title: Postdoctoral Research Assistant
Grade: Grade 6, up to point 28
Faculty/Department: Psychology
Reports to, and supervised by: Professor Dianne Berry
Responsible for: Not applicable

Purpose

To carry out research on an ESRC project grant on the relationship between implicit and explicit memory

Main duties and responsibilities

1 To familiarize yourself with the relevant literature on implicit and explicit memory
2 To recruit participants who will be needed for the project
3 To work with the programmer to ensure that the experimental programmes are appropriate for the experimental designs

4   To test participants and collate data
5   To analyse data
6   To contribute towards the writing of publications and other dissemination activities.

Terms and conditions

This post is full-time, fixed-term for 2 years. Some travel required and over-night stays away for workshops and conferences. There are no specified hours of work, but you will be required to work such hours as are necessary to carry out the duties associated with the post. Overtime is not payable.

This document outlines the duties required for the time being of the post to indicate the level of responsibility. It is not a comprehensive or exhaustive list and the line manager may vary duties from time to time which do not change the general character of the job or the level of responsibility entailed.

Date assessed: 1 March 2009

Table 10.1 Example person specification for a postdoctoral research assistant

Post title	Postdoctoral Research Assistant in Psychology	
Criteria	*Essential*	*Desirable*
Skills required	A PhD in Psychology	
Attainment	Ability to conduct laboratory experiments and analyse data appropriately	Ability to program computers in Visual Basic
Knowledge	Knowledge of cognitive psychology and studies in human memory Knowledge of multivariate statistics	Knowledge of the literature on implicit and explicit memory
Relevant experience	Experience of running laboratory experiments Experience of using multivariate statistical analysis Experience of SPSS	Experience of using statistical regression techniques
Disposition	A strong motivation for research and an ability to work well with others. Good oral and written communication skills	

There are sometimes unanticipated hold-ups when recruiting new staff, which result in delays to the start of the agreed programme of work. To take account of this, most funding organizations allow grant holders to extend the duration (but not amount of funding) of the award (normally up to a maximum of six months). Such extensions may also be requested to cover for when key staff employed on the project have periods of maternity, paternity, or paid sick leave exceeding three months. If you need to extend your award for any of the above reasons, you should talk to your institution's Research Development or Finance Office in the first instance.

It is also usually possible, if needed, to transfer awards either between different individuals within an institution or between different institutions (when the grant-holder moves from one organization to another). The former situation is less common, but may occur in the case of serious illness or other significant change of personal circumstances. The funding organization will need to be reassured that the proposed alternative grant-holder is eligible to hold the award and has the necessary expertise and experience to lead the project. The latter situation is more common, given staff mobility. Where this occurs, the 'receiving' institution must be one that is eligible to hold grants and must be able to provide the necessary supportive environment. Written agreement will be needed from both the relinquishing and the receiving organizations, which covers arrangements for the transfer of any staffing, equipment and remaining funding.

Project management

To meet project goals, lead investigators will have to exert good leadership as well as management skills. A number of different leadership styles and skills have been discussed in the literature, and are outlined below. As far as project management is concerned, the lead investigator is responsible for employing staff, and then for managing their work and their skills and career development. The amount of day to day management of staff that is required will depend on their experience level and on whether or not they form part of a larger research grouping with more experienced staff who might share in the management process. In general, project leaders do not need to know all the technical aspects of the day to day project activities. However, as Ries and Leukefeld (1998) note, they do need to know what each employee is doing, how they are doing it, what results are expected and what problems may arise. In all cases, staff need clarity on what their role is and what duties are expected of them. These should fall out of the job description. Staff should also know what explicit targets, if any, they are expected to meet and by when. There is no inherently right or wrong way to manage people. However, you should try to ensure that staff working on your projects feel valued and supported. You should convey enthusiasm and interest in their work, which at some stages of a project may appear repetitive and tedious. Recognition of even small successes is important, as non-recognition can fuel employee discontent, as noted by Ries and Leukefeld (1998). It is important that you try to see things from the perspective of your staff, and appreciate that their perspective might be different from your own, or from that of any research students you have supervised. For some research staff, working on your project is simply a job, not a career. They are prepared to work conscientiously on your project for their set hours, but do not expect to do more than this or to let the project encroach on any other aspects of their lives.

At the start of a project, the lead investigator needs to meet with project staff to overview the structure of the project and the proposed way forward. This should be followed by regular project meetings, usually held at least weekly. These will discuss progress to date, and any problems that have occurred or are anticipated to occur. Where projects involve external partners, progress meetings are likely to be scheduled at longer intervals (say, monthly or bi-monthly). As projects progress, routine meetings will also cover matters relating to producing publications and other forms of dissemination. In the second half of the project, they may also cover plans for applying for follow-up funding, if appropriate, and/or for knowledge transfer activities. Some larger projects may also involve meetings of steering committees or advisory panels, which may be scheduled, say, twice-yearly, to review the overall direction the project is taking and to comment on future direction.

It is also the responsibility of lead investigators to ensure that the research is conducted in an appropriate way, and in compliance with the institution's, and funding organization's, policies. Most institutions will have developed Codes of Good Practice in Research, or equivalent documents. These will set out the standards of performance and conduct expected of all of those engaged in research within the organization. Many of the UK Research Councils have signed up to a Joint Code of Conduct for Research (see Chapter 8), which sets out the obligations of those who are funded by them to conduct research. Researchers need to be aware of any such relevant documents and their contents. They also need to ensure that the research is conducted in line with the appropriate, and any agreed, ethical standards and procedures. As noted in Chapters 7 and 8, many research projects require approval from an appropriate REC before the work can begin. It is important to ensure that, once a project has begun, the actual work is conducted in line with what was specified in the ethical approval documentation.

As a lead researcher, you must also ensure that proper records are maintained in the form of lab notebooks, field notebooks, experimental log books, progress notes and other research related documentation. These should record the methods/procedures followed, the results obtained, and thoughts, comments and interim conclusions reached. Records should be of sufficient clarity and quality to allow the work to be repeated if necessary, and should be stored safely. It is also the responsibility of the lead researcher to ensure the appropriate storage of any research data, in line with any requirements of the funding organization. It should be noted that, within the UK, any data containing details of individuals must comply with the requirements of the Data Protection Act. The appropriate period for retaining data depends on the research area. In many areas of science, for example, it may be for a period of between five and ten years. All electronic records and data must be backed up regularly and securely.

Finally, as a lead investigator, you will have responsibility for managing the project budget and for ensuring that spending on the project is in line with the set budget. You should note that any equipment and services will have to be purchased in line with your institution's purchasing policy and guidelines. This may require getting a number of quotes from different providers to ensure that you are getting 'value for money'.

Managing staff development

As lead investigator you will also have responsibility to any staff you employ, in terms of supporting their skills and career development. This requires you to assess their development needs and to discuss with them how these might best be met. Many institutions now have dedicated Staff Training and Development departments that offer a range of training and other career development events. In some cases, researchers may require specific skills training that can only be provided by an external organization. This can be costly so you will have to see if your institution has a budget to cover such training provision, if this has not been included in the overall project budget. Researchers must also be given the opportunity to attend key conferences and meetings so that they can develop appropriate networks. Clearly, there can sometimes be tensions between pressures to deliver a fixed programme of work, necessary for the satisfactory completion of the research project, to an agreed timetable, and allowing staff sufficient time for their training and development. If you are uncertain about what an appropriate balance might be, you should seek advice from your Head of Department.

The UK Research Councils, and other major funding organizations, are committed to ensuring that any staff employed on projects they fund are offered appropriate skills training and career development opportunities. Many of these funders require grant applicants to formulate plans for supporting such training and development, when applying for funding, and ask referees to comment on these. As noted above, lead investigators will also need to comment in their final grant reports on what training and development opportunities have been taken up by staff employed on their projects. Since 2004, the Research Councils have provided ring-fenced 'Roberts Funding' to institutions to support the skills training and career development of postdoctoral research staff working on Research Council funded projects (at around £800 per year per researcher). Institutions in receipt of such funding are committed to providing appropriate training and development opportunities. The Government is committed to providing such funding until 2011, at which time the scheme is being reviewed.

The Research Councils and other major research funders in the UK are also signatories to the Concordat to support the career development of researchers. The most recent version of this was published in 2008 (www.researchconcordat.ac.uk). The Concordat is an agreement between the funders and the employers of researchers in the UK. You will need to consult your Human Resources department about how the Concordat has been implemented within your institution. The Concordat sets out a vision of working practices, roles and responsibilities to further the attractiveness and sustainability of research careers in the UK. The seven key principles that underlie it are as follows:

- There is recognition of the importance of recruiting, selecting and retaining researchers with the highest potential to achieve excellence in research.
- Researchers are recognized and valued by their employing organization as an essential part of their organization's human resources and a key component of their overall strategy to develop and deliver world class research.
- Researchers are equipped and supported to be adaptable and flexible in an increasingly diverse, mobile, global research environment.
- The importance of researchers' personal and career development, and life-long learning, is clearly recognized and promoted at all stages of their career.
- Individual researchers share the responsibility for and need to proactively engage in their own personal and career development and lifelong learning.
- Diversity and equality must be promoted in all aspects of the recruitment and career management of researchers.
- The sector and all stakeholders will undertake regular and collective review of their progress in strengthening the attractiveness and sustainability of research careers in the UK.

If you manage research staff in the UK you should also be aware of the Vitae Programme, which is supported by Government and dedicated to realizing the potential of researchers. Its website includes resources to support research managers in supporting the training and career development of their staff.

Leadership styles and skills

The principal investigator (PI) is not only the project manager but also the intellectual leader. As Ball (2007) notes, for academic research, leadership usually involves giving a group of people a clear vision and a clear sense of direction, trying to take them forward, as a collective and as individuals, in that direction and initiating appropriate actions. Put more simply, this involves engaging people in the research agenda and stimulating or enthusing them. Several researchers and commentators have published generic guidelines for being an effective leader that can be applied to research leadership. Such guidelines typically include having a strong vision, developing professional expertise, cultivating enthusiasm, respecting staff and paying attention to accomplishment and being accessible. Building on this, Burman and Evans (2008) published a charter for leaders, which included the following points:

- leading by example in accordance with the institution's core values;
- building the trust and confidence of people they work with;
- continually seeking improvement in methods and effectiveness;
- keeping people informed;
- being accountable for their actions and holding others accountable for theirs;
- involving people, seeking their views and listening actively to them;
- being clear on what is expected and providing feedback on progress;
- showing tolerance of people's differences and dealing with their issues fairly;
- acknowledging and recognizing people for their contributions and performance;
- weighing alternatives, considering both short and long term effects and being resolute in the decisions they make.

Whatever the nature and size of group that academic researchers lead, many of the above guidelines and characteristics will be relevant. It is important not to take 'leadership' for granted; that is, as something that just happens when you are in a certain position. It is important to reflect on the style of leadership you are showing and consider whether there is room for improvement. It is also worth considering engaging in some training or coaching in order to enhance your leadership and team management skills. Many institutions either run, or organize, such programmes.

Research leadership on a wider front

Many successful researchers and research group leaders working within universities are asked to take on wider leadership roles. This may be at a department or school level, or across a faculty or the entire university. Such leaders, or directors, of research need to display further skills in addition to many of the leadership skills outlined above. If you take on one of these roles you will be required to direct research across a broader range of areas which, in some cases, can extend way beyond your own expertise. Clearly, such leaders do not require a detailed understanding of all such research areas in order to direct research appropriately. However, you do have to have a broad level of understanding of what the research involves, and what is required to support it, and have an open mind towards research styles and traditions that may be very different from those of your own discipline. Ball (2007) notes that good research leadership is important for the advancement of research in universities. Thus, universities may enable the achievement of research outputs and objectives through the recognition of the need for, and promotion of, research leadership, and also through the realization that academics believe that it is feasible to lead research.

A key aspect of this broader leadership is to motivate researchers to apply for research funding, and to use appropriate sources of help and advice. Many institutions set specific targets for individuals, or research groups, in terms of the number of grant applications they submit per year, or the number of grant awards they should hold at any time. To do this, it is necessary to have good statistical and management information, looking at the current and past levels of performance, and comparing these with the performance of competitor groups and institutions. There are a number of routinely published sources of information that can be used to find out about the research of other universities (at least in the UK). These include the annual statistics produced by HESA, and the annual reports and summary analyses published by the Research Councils and other major funders. In addition, a company called Evidence UK produces an annual yearbook that is an excellent source of information about the performance of your own institution in comparison with others. Finally, HEFCE makes available the majority of the information that was collected as part of the RAE, via the RAE 2008 website.

Estimating and setting research-related targets in an informed way, so that they are meaningful to the research or research group, is not easy. It is very important that the researchers themselves feel ownership of any targets that are set, or the targets are unlikely to be effective. Determining what actions to take when performance falls short of targets is another difficult issue. Most researchers, however, will respond better to incentives and rewards than to threats and punishments. Many institutions 'reward' successful grant winners by allocating them a share of any 'overhead' or equivalent income they bring in (either as a salary payment or as an allowance that they can use in any way to support their future research). Having access to such funding can be exceedingly useful for researchers, in that it gives them more freedom and flexibility in terms of paying for casual labour, buying additional equipment, or supporting travel. Many academic departments will also have in place workload models that take account of research project management when allocating other workload. So successful grant winners may find that they get allocated smaller teaching and administrative loads. Finally, many departments or universities will operate internal funding schemes to support small pump-priming projects, which are aimed at incentivizing researchers and putting them in a stronger position to compete successfully for external funding.

In addition to motivating researchers to apply for funding and produce strong applications, research leaders also have to encourage researchers to take on more altruistic roles, such as acting as research mentors to more junior colleagues, or contributing towards internal peer review systems by providing constructive criticism of colleagues' draft proposals and research outputs.

Collaborating with others

Chapter 7 suggested a number of questions that prospective members of collaborative teams should ask themselves before deciding whether or not to join the team. Once a team has been established and has been awarded funding, it is important to ensure that the team works effectively. A good collaborative culture must be characterized by a team approach that supports flexibility and promotes mutual trust, open communication and cooperation. As Gitlin and Lyons (2008) note, developing specific and clearly defined roles is a critical aspect of the collaborative group process. It is important for the group to define key roles early in the collaboration, and match the requirements of a particular role with the expertise of particular team members. One person will need to assume the role of project leader, although this usually has to be agreed at the time of applying for funding, as most funding organizations require information about how collaborative projects will be managed if awarded. The leader must assume the overall direction of the collaborative team building effort, as well as facilitate or coordinate the work tasks of the research team. Being the lead partner usually involves a greater commitment of time than is required by other team members.

To reduce the likelihood of problems arising, collaborative groups need to establish some ground rules at the outset, which assure that divisive behaviours will not be tolerated. As Gitlin and Lyons (2008) note, the group leader needs to take control of meetings and redirect the group should any such behaviours occur. They should be modelling expected behaviours and clearly reinforcing the value of each member's ideas. Clearly it is important to ensure that al agreed project tasks are completed in accordance with the agreed timescale One strategy that you can use to help this is to circulate written lists of agreed tasks, showing who is responsible for completing them, and by when. It is also useful to develop contingency plans for renegotiating roles and areas of responsibility if there are early signs of tension.

Coping with difficulties

Most projects go to plan and proceed relatively smoothly. However, o occasions, there can be difficulties that need to be addressed and managed First, there may be difficulties simply because the work does not progres as planned; experiments do not work, recruitment of specialist participant populations does not go according to schedule; access to key resources is not provided, and so on. Your planned timescale should allow for some minor hold-ups. However, in some instances, you might need to revise project objectives and future work plans to take account of such unanticipated difficulties.

Alternatively, difficulties can arise as a result of tensions and differences of opinion between different project partners. As Heller (2002) notes, most team problems are caused by a breakdown in trust. This might stem from one or more of the partners not delivering their parts of the work on the agreed timescale. Gitlin and Lyons (2008) suggest that problems can occur at the individual, group dynamic or institution level. In the former case, members might show divisive working behaviours that impede group work, for example if particular team members ridicule ideas or take an overall negative approach to suggestions made by others. Some team members simply start to lose interest in projects, as a result of changes in their own priorities and goals. At the group level, problems can arise in relation to differences of opinion about how best to proceed or tackle a particular issue. Difficulties can also arise as a result of different project partners (particularly when from different disciplinary backgrounds) not sharing a similar 'vocabulary' and style of working. Finally, problems can arise as a result of institutional level changes in personnel or priorities. Some difficulties and tensions, such as those arising from when a team member has not kept to an agreed time schedule, can be addressed openly in project planning meetings, and a method for resolving them should be discussed and agreed between partners, if possible. Sometimes this will require the lead partner to show firm leadership and direction. If a partner fails to deliver to such an extent that the project could be at risk, the lead partner may need to discuss removing, and possibly replacing, the partner, with the funding organization. Other problems may require the team leader to discuss issues on a one-to-one basis with particular team members.

Finally, difficulties might relate to dissatisfaction with the performance, behaviour, or attitudes, of one or more of the staff employed on the project. Heller (2002: 185) lists seven 'golden rules' for dealing with problems with staff you manage:

Be firm but scrupulously fair.
Be clear and honest.
Be constructive in your comments and suggestions.
Always look for a positive outcome and encourage others to do so.
Take action early – do not put things off and let problems grow.
Document discussions and actions.
Remain calm.

In the first instance, you should meet with the staff member or members to discuss your concerns in an open and civilized way. You should ensure that there is clarity and agreement about what their expected role and duties are, as well as what is normally considered to be an acceptable standard of behaviour. You should make sure that the staff member has opportunity and encouragement to express their views. If issues cannot be resolved at a one-to-one level, you many need to consult your Head of Department or Human Resources department for further advice. Most institutions require staff to be given clear warning, in writing, of any dissatisfaction in performance, and an opportunity to address this, before moving to a stage of dismissing the member of staff concerned. Where the staff member concerned is new to the organization, there is likely to be a set probationary period to their employment. It is much better (and easier) to address any such employment issues during the probationary period, rather than at a later stage if employment continues beyond the probationary period. A large number of books and other resources have been published to help managers to 'manage' their staff. Some of these are listed in Appendix 1 (p. 159).

Building and sustaining a team

Bushaway (2003) proposes that most researchers have a clear idea of the size and composition of the research team necessary for success in their fields. Group Dynamic Theory tends to indicate that around 10 individuals, bringing a balance of skills to the task, makes an effective team, but the university must be flexible enough to encourage groups to form, grow, change, interact, decline, transform and reform as fluidly as possible, on the basis of research performance measured against objective benchmarks. Bringing together a group of people does not necessarily mean that they will function effectively as a team. As Heller (2002: 173) notes, a successful team needs:

- a diversity of membership;
- common and challenging goals;
- involvement of team members;
- good communications.

All team members must know exactly what they are expected to achieve at a number of levels. According to Heller (2002: 173), you will need to:

- develop a team vision and goals;
- ensure that every team member knows what to do to contribute to team goals;
- review how team goals relate to wider organizational goals.

An important point to remember is that you should not simply rely on 'team management' to the exclusion of individual person management. You need to take time to meet with each team member, and to treat them as individuals as well as part of a team. You also need to recognize the different goals and motivations of different team members. Many teams, for example, will include a combination of research assistants/fellows and postgraduate research students. It is important to provide the appropriate types of supervision and support to the different types of group member.

The type of research team you should build will depend, to some extent, on the disciplinary area within which you work. In some cases, a research team might simply consist of three or four postdoctoral researchers and a similar number of postgraduate research students, all working on their own individual project within a common general area. In other cases, the team members will have different roles: some may be researchers but others may be scientific officers, technicians, clerical staff, and so on. Additionally, more than one researcher might work on any one particular project, with the different researchers taking on different roles, as appropriate for their skills and level of experience. Once your team gets to a certain size, it is important to ensure that there is at least one or more senior member who can help you to manage less experienced staff, produce outputs and formulate new funding proposals.

As you build your research team, you also need to think about how to sustain it. Most research projects run for a period of between one year and five years. If you want to retain a good member of your research team, it is important to ensure that there is a funded project for them to move on to when their current project ends. Given the length of time it takes to develop a competitive application, and the possibility of being rejected first time round, you need to start to work on any follow-on proposals at least a year before the current project ends. You can see why successful researchers, who are more advanced in their career, prefer to apply for longer programme grants which offer more stability and more opportunity to deliver on the current programme of work before having to think about funding the next.

One way to help ensure the sustainability of your research group is to try to achieve a diversity of funding. This helps to protect you from some of the 'vagaries of fashion' in research funding. Researchers need to obtain the right balance between establishing a relationship with a core funder, through a repeated history of funding, and broadening their funding base to prevent the risk of unexpected changes in mission and priorities of one particular funder. A successful team, for example, might be funded by a large British Heart Foundation (BHF) programme grant, an MRC project grant, two BHF research studentships, and an award from the pharmaceutical industry.

Shaping the funding agenda

One way to increase your chances of being successful when applying for research funding is to be in a position to contribute to shaping the agenda of the funding organization. Being part of a key committee, board or advisory college for a funding organization gives you more opportunity to understand the priorities and ways of thinking of the organization and allows you to contribute towards their future strategic planning. Members of committees and boards are often asked to generate ideas for new funding initiatives for example. In addition, they will often hear about new funding schemes before calls for proposals are made available to the wider research community. This allows more time for generating ideas for potential proposals, discussing these with potential collaborators if team based research is required, and formulating research plans and study designs. This is important as announcements for new funding opportunities often have relatively short deadlines by which outlines or proposals have to be submitted.

Most major funding organizations select new committee members using a very transparent process. The UK Research Councils call for nominations, annually, to fill vacancies that will be arising on their committees as a result of member turnover. You should keep an eye on their websites for such calls. Funding organizations will select appropriate new members from those who have been nominated, depending on the area of expertise of the nominees and how this matches what is needed on the committee. They will also take account of needing to have a sufficiently diverse panel in terms of gender, institution and location. Nominees who are known to the funding organization, usually as a result of holding grants funded by the organization and being on peer review colleges, and so on, are more likely to be selected. In addition, funding organizations are likely to look at how well prospective committee members have disseminated their work; whether they have a record of producing high quality publications and other outputs.

Some funding organizations also develop closer relationships with particular institutions, and may 'sound out' these institutions when thinking about introducing new funding schemes. EPSRC, for example, has recently identified a number (currently 12) of 'framework universities'. These are universities that have received more than a certain amount of EPSRC research income, and have a larger portfolio of projects. The University Framework agreements do not provide extra funding to the universities in question, but do give them some flexibility over how they can use their existing EPSRC funding and give them a voice in relation to EPSRC's strategic planning. Activities engaged in with Framework Universities include:

- sharing data and information;
- cooperating in managing research and training;

- identifying opportunities for increased knowledge transfer from EPSRC funded research;
- jointly promoting the interests of researchers and building the case for public funding of engineering and physical sciences.

Dissemination

Effective dissemination of research is clearly important for all researchers, not just those seeking to become members of funding organizations' committees. We saw in Chapter 7 that most funding organizations require applicants to outline their plans for disseminating the proposed research when applying for funding, and these plans are taken into account by referees and assessors. Clearly an important form of dissemination for most researchers is through publications. In many cases, this will be in the form of internationally recognized journal articles, but may include books and book chapters, and conference papers. In the case of more applied projects, outputs may include technical reports, policy papers, computer software, databases and patents. Most researchers will also want to disseminate their work to their peers at appropriate conferences and scientific meetings.

Publishing in the academic literature

Just as it is important to gain funding to support and sustain research programmes and teams, it is also important to disseminate the outcomes of the research that is carried out as part of projects. Funding bodies will always look at the track record of applicants when determining whether or not to award funding. This involves looking at the amount and quality of outputs produced by the applicant and, where relevant, how well the applicant has disseminated the outcomes of previously funded research. Most researchers will already be familiar with the publication process before starting to apply for their first research grant. This is because many are encouraged to publish the outcomes of their PhD, and/or postdoctoral projects on which they have worked. At this early stage of career, such publications are often written in collaboration with a more senior author (such as a supervisor or PI). As you progress in your career you are more likely to become the lead author, particularly where publications are associated with projects on which you have been the PI. It is important to adopt a responsible attitude to ensuring that any associated research students or assistants are given full credit for their contributions to projects when publishing outcomes. Most academic journals have authorship policies which provide guidance about who should, and who should not, be named as an author, depending on the level of contribution to the research in question. When the contribution is too slight to warrant authorship, an acknowledgement to the contribution is usually provided in the appropriate section of the publication.

Just as there is increasing pressure on research staff to gain research funding for research, so is there pressure to publish high quality outputs. As we saw in Chapter 1, research assessment processes (such as the RAE and REF in the UK) are primarily concerned with assessing the quality of research outputs. As a researcher it is important to be mindful of the 'quality' of the potential outlet you choose for publishing your work, looking, for example, at the impact factors of scientific journals (which reflect how much on average articles published in the journal have been cited by other researchers). It is important, however, to take account of a number of factors when selecting an appropriate outlet. This will include the overall perceived quality of the research in question, the audiences you want to reach, the acceptance rate of the journal or publisher, and the length of time the publication process is likely to take (including the length of delay between acceptance of the work and actual publication). It is sometimes important for you to get new findings published quickly, or to ensure that more junior staff or associated students get one or two publications quickly so that they can be more competitive in the jobs market or when applying for funding in their own names. In such cases, you may choose to submit work to outlets that are known to publish accepted work within a relatively short time of it being submitted.

Concerns over ensuring that staff publish high quality outputs have led many universities and research groups to introduce a system of internal peer review of publications, whereby draft publications are read and commented on by more experienced researchers prior to submission. Such researchers will also provide advice on appropriate journals, publishers and other publication outlets.

Other forms of dissemination

Many of the above forms of dissemination relate to academic audiences, but it is also important to disseminate your research findings to appropriate non-academic audiences where this is appropriate. This may involve writing for trade magazines or other such documents read by practitioners and policy makers. It may also involve speaking at meetings where such people will be present. Major research funding organizations, like the Research Councils, expect grant applicants to include plans for dissemination to any relevant non-academic audiences, in addition to academic audiences, when submitting proposals, and ask reviewers and assessors to comment on these. Where relevant, they also expect non-academic users to be involved, at some level, when they are developing and carrying out projects.

In addition, researchers are increasingly being encouraged to contribute to public engagement activities. Several of the Research Councils offer specific grants to support 'public understanding of science' or other public engagement activities. EPSRC, for example, runs a Partnerships for Public Engagement scheme, with the aim of communicating the excitement of fundamental and applied research in science and engineering to the wider public. To improve standards of public engagement activities, the council also allows applicants to request additional funding to support communications training. In addition to the schemes run by the individual Research Councils, the Department for Innovation, Universities and Skills funds Science Wise, which is an expert resource centre for public dialogue in science and innovation to support and encourage ways of making science accessible to public audiences in the UK. It aims to help policy makers commission and use public dialogue to inform policy decisions in emerging areas of science and technology by commissioning and funding public engagement projects. Similarly, the British Science Association (formerly British Association for the Advancement of Science) supports a number of awards and schemes to facilitate the advance of science and its public understanding.

The need to disseminate and promote research outputs has encouraged many institutions (as well as disciplinary based bodies and associations) to develop publications repositories, that store details about all of the research outputs of their staff, with links to the full text or copies of the full text itself where available. Some publishers will allow researchers to lodge copies of their research outputs in such institutional or disciplinary focused repositories without infringing copyright agreements, but others will not. It is essential that you check your copyright agreement before lodging any outputs in open access repositories. A number of institutions are also starting to develop repositories to store research data and other related materials. Research funding organizations are now starting to require applicants for research funding to state how their data will be stored and how they will provide access to it by other researchers. The ESRC, for example, has a long-standing data archive based at Essex University. Before submitting proposals, applicants are required to check the archive to ensure that a duplicate, or very similar, data set has not already been collected and deposited and, if not, to determine whether the data they propose to collect will be suitable for depositing in the archive. ESRC expects all grant holders to offer for deposit both machine-readable, and non-machine readable qualitative data to the archive within three months of the end of projects. The data must be deposited to a standard which would enable the data to be used by a third party, including the provision of adequate documentation. ESRC may withhold the final payment of the award if data is not deposited to the required standard and within three months of the end of the project, except where a waiver of deposit has been agreed in advance.

In today's competitive environment, it is increasingly important for researchers to be 'known'. If you have particularly significant findings you should contact your institution's press office so that they can help you to prepare an appropriate media release. You should also ensure that your department and personal web pages are updated with details of key new findings and recent publications, so that they can be picked up by relevant search engines.

Collaborating with industry

One way of ensuring good user engagement, and to increase the diversity of your funding base, is to involve a 'user' either as the primary research funder or as a collaborative partner. It is important to appreciate, however, that while bringing many potential advantages, collaborating with commercial and industrial partners can raise issues and tensions. As the Lambert Review (Lambert 2003: 79) notes

> In many ways, businesses and universities do not make easy bedfellows. They have different values and different missions. They work on different timescales and towards different objectives under different management systems. Building a culture that allows the two to come together in a creative fashion requires considerable commitment from both sides, and an infrastructure that can sustain the relationship.

Overall, there is a lack of knowledge about potential partners and about possibilities for interaction, on both sides of the exchange. Zinser (1985) notes that as a university moves closer to partnerships with industry it may relinquish some of its unique capabilities for unrestricted exploratory research and freedom of action. She considers that these partnerships with industry can lead to universities shifting from basic research to applied research and product development, to a reduction in academic freedom, a compromise of academic integrity, a constraint on the timely dissemination of research results and to a limitation of choice in selecting research topics.

There are a number of benefits, however, for both parties in forming collaborations between businesses and universities. As Prigge (2005) notes, for universities, these benefits include financial support, broadening the experience of staff and students and identification of interesting problems. Other non-pecuniary benefits include access to data, facilities and equipment and corporate intelligence and market knowledge. For businesses, potential benefits include access to expertise that they do not have in-house, the ability to expand pre-competitive research, helping in the renewal and expansion of their technology, and access to potential employees. Interaction with university academics may also enable a company to identify issues of which it was previously unaware. Valentin (2000) breaks down university benefits into three categories:

- *financial* which includes new financial resources and obtaining public grants;
- *technological* which includes access to the firm's equipment and materials as well as access to the firm's employment, scientific and technological experience;
- *strategic* which includes scientific breakthroughs and progress, as well as access to industry's managerial experience.

The key point is that when considering forming collaborations with businesses, you need to consider carefully the ways in which you expect to benefit, and how this compares with any potential costs. According to Cyert and Goodman (1997: 51), 'the basic functions of a University are to create new knowledge and disseminate existing knowledge. Relationships with industries should be formed only if one or both of these functions are expected. The alliance should not be entered into merely as a way to finance research'. To make an alliance a success, both parties need to be prepared to adapt to each other's requirements and cultures.

Skingle (2000) lists four issues that academics should consider before approaching a prospective industrial collaborator:

- Is the industrial scientist likely to make a significant intellectual contribution to the project?
- Does the company have a good track record for collaborations with academia?
- Does the industrial scientist have access to knowledge or technology which may contribute towards the aims of the proposed research?
- Is the industrial partner well placed to exploit intellectual property arising from the collaboration in an efficient and effective way?

Skingle notes that the vast majority of academic collaborations funded by GlaxoSmith Kline happen as a result of a proactive discussion between an industrial and an academic scientist. Often the academic will be aware of the company's potential research interests and may contact the industrial scientist at a conference or via email. In general, a short conversation or email exchange will determine whether it is worth taking a potential collaboration further and developing a proposal for funding.

Prior to any joint activity occurring, both sides of the potential collaboration need to spend some time identifying the ways in which they would benefit from working together, and how the collaboration would actually be carried out and supported. This will inevitably be a learning experience for both parties. Most joint projects result from a series of interactions between the two partners, although occasionally one party might fully conceive of a project before approaching the potential partner. Interestingly, it is usually 'contact between individuals' rather than institutional relationships that dominate the opening phases of university–business interactions (Abreu et al. 2008).

There is considerable variation in the extent to which academics are involved in knowledge exchange activities with the business sector. A study by D'Este and Patel (2007) shows that, while 30 per cent of EPSRC grant holders had no interaction, over 50 per cent interact using three or more modes (e.g. contract research, consultancy, joint research training, development of facilities). Although there has traditionally been more exchange activity in science and engineering based disciplines, business is increasingly placing emphasis on getting social science inputs (e.g. Brown 2007; Abreu et al. 2008). There are clearly a number of different ways in which experienced researchers can collaborate with business and industry. Some of these were considered in Chapter 4, when looking at the funding of research grants and contracts and research fellowships. In addition to these, many experienced researchers may be asked to provide some form of research consultancy to particular organizations. Some of these researchers may be working independently but many will be based in HEIs. Most universities allow (and even encourage) academic staff to carry out up to a set amount of consultancy each year, and have developed policies to provide guidance on how the resulting income should be shared between the researcher and the institution.

Commercial exploitation

In some areas, it may be appropriate to take knowledge transfer a step further and to engage in some form of commercial exploitation of your research. There are a number of issues to consider in doing this, such as how 'close to market' the 'product' is, the strength of any IP protection, the potential market for the 'product', the wishes of the researcher/team, and the resources of the host institution. The most appropriate and effective model for commercial exploitation of intellectual property arising from research needs to be considered on a case by case basis. Typically, one (or more) of the following would be used:

- IP licence or assignment, in return for revenue payments (such as annual royalties);
- IP licence or assignment, in return for a one-off lump sum payment or up-front fee, or shares in the buying entity;
- the formation of a company, generally referred to as a 'spin-out company', by the host institution in which it will hold shares and to which the IP is licensed and/or assigned.

Licensing tends to be the more appropriate route to commercialization in cases where the 'product' is close to market, there is an existing company with the desire and resources to bring the product to market, or the host institution does not have the resources to support a spin-out company. To bring a new drug candidate to market, for example, requires significant investments of resource in addition to detailed understanding of regulatory requirements. Formation of a spin-out company may be a more appropriate route to commercialization if the 'product' requires further development that is capable of being done by the researcher and if the 'product' has broad application (and could potentially become multiple products).

Since around 2005, many universities have established technology transfer, or similar, offices to support the commercial exploitation of research. You should contact such offices at the earliest stage if you are considering any form of commercial exploitation.

It is the policy of the UK Research Councils (and some other major research funders) that potentially valuable results or products arising from research they have funded should, where practicable, be fully exploited. To facilitate this, four of the councils (NERC, EPSRC, BBSRC and STFC) have introduced a 'proof of concept' or 'follow-on' fund to support the commercialization of ideas arising from research. The purpose of the funding is to help scientists to develop research ideas to a stage where commercialization opportunities, such as licensing, can be secured. Funds can support further scientific and technical development of an idea, though applications may involve some activities towards improving an intellectual property position, market research, or investigating potential licensees and joint ventures. Applications should be sent to the Research Council that funded the original piece of research and must build on the outcomes of that research. There are two specific schemes to which researchers can apply:

- *Follow-on Fund pathfinder.* This supports small-scale, specific activities that can help develop a better understanding of future work needs and may be beneficial when submitting a full Follow-on Fund application. Up to £20 000 can be sought through this scheme to carry out work that will help researchers to develop a greater understanding of the commercial aspects or possibilities of their research.
- *Follow-on Fund.* This is the main scheme, with no limit on the amount of funding that can be sought. However, as support is only provided for a maximum of 12 months, the amount sought should be reasonable according to the work to be carried out (with grants normally being around £80 000 to £100 000).

Final words

Clearly, there are many ways in which you as a researcher can move on to become a successful manager and leader of research, engage in collaborations and work with commercial partners to secure a larger portfolio of funded research, if you are motivated to do so. It is important to note that, when building a research career, success tends to give rise to further success. Experienced researchers with large, well-funded research programmes will typically have a track record of successful applications starting from the earliest stages of their career. Many will also have played a role in shaping the funding agenda, by being invited to join grants panels and other key bodies.

Applying for, and gaining, research funding, from the earliest stages, is important for all the reasons outlined at the start of this book. If you are successful, it will help you to be more productive and to establish yourself as a leading researcher. However, it is important to remember that securing funding must always be considered to be the 'means', as opposed to the end result. It is the research itself, and the associated outcomes, and the fulfilment you feel when discovering new knowledge, that are the real drivers.

APPENDIX 1

Additional Resources

Chapter 1

An overall useful source of information is HERO: the official gateway to universities, colleges and research organizations in the UK (www.hero.ac.uk)

UK Higher Education Funding Councils

HEFCE   Higher Education Funding Council for England
www.hefce.ac.uk
HEFCW   Higher Education Funding Council for Wales
www.hefcw.ac.uk
DENI   Department of Education for Northern Ireland
www.deni.gov.uk
SFC   Scottish Funding Council
www.sfc.ac.uk

Chapter 2

Research Councils UK
www.rcuk.ac.uk

Chapter 3

UK Research Councils

AHRC   Arts and Humanities Research Council
www.ahrc.ac.uk
BBSRC   Biotechnology and Biological Sciences Research Council
www.bbsrc.ac.uk
EPSRC   Engineering and Physical Sciences Research Council
www.epsrc.ac.uk
ESRC   Economic and Social Research Council
www.esrc.ac.uk
MRC   Medical Research Council
www.mrc.ac.uk
NERC   Natural Environment Research Council
STFC   Science and Technology Facilities Council
www.stfc.ac.uk

Chapter 4

UK Professional Associations

British Academy: The UK's National Academy for the Humanities and Social
Sciences
www.britac.ac.uk
Royal Society: The UK's National Academy of Science
www.royalsociety.org

Trusts and Charities

The Leverhulme Trust
www.leverhulme.ac.uk
The Nuffield Foundation
www.nuffieldfoundation.org
The Joseph Rowntree Foundation
www.jrf.org
The Wellcome Trust
www.wellcome.ac.uk
Alzheimer's Research Trust
www.alzheimers-research.org.uk
British Heart Foundation
www.bhf.org.uk

Cancer Research UK
  www.cancerresearchuk.org
Parkinson's Disease Society
  www.parkinsons.org.uk
Association of Medical Research Charities
  www.amrc.org.uk

UK Government Departments and related bodies

BERR   Department for Business, Enterprise and Regulatory Reform
  www.berr.gov.uk
DOH   Department of Health
  www.doh.gov.uk
DEFRA   Department for Environment, Food and Rural Affairs
  www.defra.gov.uk
DIUS   Department for Innovation, Universities and Skills
  www.dius.gov.uk
DOT   Department of Transport
  www.dot.gov.uk
DELNI   Department for Employment and Learning, Northern Ireland
  www.delni.gov.uk
DSTL   Defence Science and Technology Laboratory
  www.dstl.gov.uk
QinetiQ
  www.qinetiq.com
National Institute for Health Research
  www.nihr.ac.uk
Technology Strategy Board
  www.innovateuk.org

Overseas funding organizations

The European Commission
  www.ec.europa.uk
CORDIS   Community Research and Development Information Service (A
  better source of information on EU funding for UK researchers)
  www.cordis.lu/en/home
UK Research Office
  www.ukro.ac.uk
NATO Science Programme
  www.nato.int/science
National Science Foundation
  www.nsf.gov

Chapter 5

Joint Electronic Submission system (Je-S)
www.je-s.rcuk.ac.uk
MRC Electronic Application system
www.eaa.mrc.ac.uk

Chapter 6

An overall useful guide for early career researchers is a 2009 publication by Alan Johnson *Charting a Course for a Successful Research Career* (see reference section for further details).

ResearchResearch (Electronic version of Research Fortnight publication)
www.ResearchResearch.com
COS Community of Science
www.cos.com
Missenden Centre for the Development of Higher Education
www.missendencentre.co.uk

Grants Schemes for new researchers

EPSRC First Grants scheme and Challenging Engineering Scheme
www.epsrc.ac.uk/researchfunding/opportunities/newacademics
BBSRC New Investigators scheme
www.bbsrc.ac.uk/funding/grants/new_investigator.html
MRC New Investigator research grants
www.mrc.ac.uk/fundingopportunities/grants/NIRG/index.htm
NERC New Investigator research grant
www.nerc.ac.uk/funding/available/researchgrants/typesofaward/
newinvestigators.asp
AHRC route for Early Career Researchers
www.ahrc.ac.uk/fundingopportunities/pages/rg-earlycareers.aspx

Fellowship schemes for Early Career Researchers

EPSRC Postdoctoral Fellowship scheme
www.epsrc.ac.uk/researchfunding/opportunities/fellowships/
postdoctoralfellowships.htm
NERC Early Career Development awards
www.nerc.ac.uk/funding/available/fellowships/typesofaward.asp

MRC Career Development awards
www.mrc.ac.uk/fundingopportunities/fellowships/
careerdevelopmentaward/index.htm
BBSRC David Phillips Fellowships
www.bbsrc.ac.uk/funding/fellowships/david_phillips.html
AHRC Research Fellowships (Early Career Researcher strand)
www.ahrc.ac.uk/fundingopportunities/fellowships/aspx
Wellcome Trust Sir Henry Wellcome PhD Fellowships and Research Career
Development Fellowships
www.wellcome.ac.uk/funding/biomedical-science/grants/fellowships-and-
personal-awards/basic-biomedical-fellowships.index.htm
British Academy Postdoctoral Fellowship scheme
www.britac.ac.uk/funding/guide/pdfells.cfm
Leverhulme Early Career Fellowships
www.leverhulme.ac.uk/grants_awards/grants/early_career_fellowships/

Chapter 7

Electronic resources for literature searches

Web of Knowledge
www.isi.webofknowledge.com
WorldCat
www.worldcat.org
Google Scholar
www.scholar.google.co.uk
Amazon books
www.amazon.co.uk

Chapter 8

Guides to good research conduct

RCUK Policy and Code of Conduct on the Governance of Good Research Conduct: Integrity, Clarity and Good Management (revised July 2009)
www.rcuk.ac.uk
BBSRC   Statement on safeguarding good scientific practice (revised 2007)
www.bbsrc.ac.uk/publications/policy/good_scientific_practice.html

EPSRC Guide to Good Practice in Science and Engineering Research
www.epsrc.ac.uk/ResearchFunding/GrantHolders/
GuideToGoodPracticeInScienceAndEngineeringResearch.htm
UK Research Integrity Office (UKRIO) Code of Practice for Research: Promoting
good practice and preventing misconduct (revised September 2009)
www.ukrio.org

Research ethics frameworks and guides

ESRC Research Ethics Framework (July 2005)
www.esrc.ac.uk/ref
NERC Ethics Policy
www.nerc.ac.uk/about/work/policy/ethics/
MRC Ethics Series. December 1997 et seq.
www.mrc.ac.uk/PolicyGuidance/EthicsAndGovernance
Universal ethical code for scientists (CST report, 2006)
www.berr.gov.uk/dius/science/science-and-society/public_engagement/
code/page28030.html

National Health Service Research Ethics Approval

National Research Ethics Service (NRES) (Includes access to the Integrated
Research Application System – IRAS)
www.nres.npsa.nhs.uk
Human Tissue Act
www.hta.gov.uk

Chapter 9

Transparent Approach to Costing and Full Economic Costing

JISC   Joint Information Systems Committee
www.jisc.ac.uk/fundingopportunities/bidguide.aspx
Joint Costing and Pricing Steering Group. Consolidated TRAC Guidance
www.jcpsg.ac.uk/guidance

Intellectual property

UK Intellectual Property Office
www.ipo.gov.uk

Chapter 10

Research Management texts

Adair, J. (2002) *100 Greatest Ideas for Effective Leadership and Management*. Chichester: Capstone.

Duke, C. (2002) *Managing the Learning University*. Society for Research in Higher Education. Maidenhead: Open University Press.

Heller, R. (ed.) (2002) *Manager's Handbook*. London: Dorling Kindersley.

McCaffery, P. (2004) *The HE Manager's Handbook: Effective Leadership and Management in Universities and Colleges*. London: Routledge Falmer.

Staff employment and development

Jobs.ac.uk (Main internet site for advertising jobs in the UK)

Research Careers Initiative. Universities UK
www.universitiesuk.ac.uk

Research Concordat
www.researchconcordat.ac.uk

Vitae. For researchers, supervisors, research managers and employers
www.vitae.ac.uk

APPENDIX 2

RCUK's six multidisciplinary priority research programmes

Energy

This £319 million programme is led by EPSRC, and also involves BBSRC, ESRC, NERC and STFC. It brings together energy related research and training across these councils to address the outstanding international issues of climate change and security of energy supply. The programme aims to sustain the strong research portfolio in power generation and supply, and grow the portfolio in demand reduction, alternative energy vectors, transport and security of supply.

Living with Environmental Change

This £363 million programme is led by NERC and involves all seven Research Councils. It is a major interdisciplinary research and policy partnership to tackle environmental change and the societal challenges it poses. The programme aims to provide the knowledge, tools, predictions and business solutions needed to increase resilience to, and reduce the economic impacts of, environmental changes such as more severe weather and reduced biodiversity, and the best information to enable sustainable management and protection of vital ecosystem services, such as clean air, fresh water and fresh soils.

Global Threats to Security

This £114 million programme is led by ESRC and again involves all seven Research Councils. It addresses four interrelated global threats to security (crime, terrorism, environmental stress and global poverty), each linked in a systematic way to address three themes – causes, detection, and possible interventions to prevent harm. The programme seeks to understand how crime, terror, environmental stress and poverty create vicious circles through positive feedback.

Ageing: Lifelong Health and Well-being

Ageing research is a longstanding priority area for the Research Councils, and this £486 million programme brings together all seven councils under the leadership of MRC. The programme provides substantial longer term funding for new interdisciplinary centres targeting themes of healthy ageing and factors over the whole life course that may be major determinants of health and well-being in later life. It embraces a number of specific research themes including quality of life, physical frailty and the ageing brain.

Digital Economy

This £58 million programme is led by EPSRC and also involves AHRC, ESRC and MRC. It focuses on areas where the management and presentation of information can have maximum transformational impact, such as healthcare, transport and the creative industries.

Nanoscience through Engineering to Application

This £51 million programme is again led by EPSRC and involves all the other Research Councils apart from AHRC. It focuses on areas of societal importance, such as energy, environmental remediation, the digital economy and healthcare, and includes studies on risk governance, economics and the social implications of nanoscience.

APPENDIX 3

Details of the 2007–11 Delivery Plans of the UK Research Councils

BBSRC

- Energy – renewable bioenergy
- Living with environmental change
- Ageing: Lifelong health and well-being
- Global threats to security
- Nanotechnology
- Embedding systems biology
- Synthetic biology
- Stem cells

MRC

- Ageing: Lifelong health and well-being
- Living with environmental change
- Digital economy
- Global threats to security
- Nanoscience
- Energy
- Translational research
- Global health
- Population science

EPSRC

- Energy
- Digital economy
- Nanoscience
- Next generation healthcare

NERC

- Living with environmental change
- Global threats to security
- Climate systems
- Biodiversity
- Sustainable use of natural resources
- Earth system science
- Natural hazards
- Environmental pollution and human health
- Technologies

ESRC

- Energy
- Living with environmental change
- Terrorism, security, global conflict and uncertainty
- Lifelong health and well-being
- Digital economy
- Nanoscience
- Succeeding in the global economy
- Migration and population change
- Understanding individual behaviour

AHRC

- Global threats to security
- Living with environmental change

- Ageing: Lifelong health and well-being
- Stimulating innovation in the knowledge economy
- Capitalising on our cultural assets

STFC

- Energy
- Living with environmental change
- Global threats to security
- Ageing: Lifelong health and well-being
- Nanoscience

APPENDIX 4

Criteria used by EPSRC to assess responsive mode applications

Please comment on the degree of excellence of the proposal, making reference to the:

- novelty, relationship to the context, and timeliness
- ambition, adventure, and transformative aspects identified
- appropriateness of the proposed methodology

For multidisciplinary proposals, please state which aspects of the proposal you feel qualified to assess.

Please comment on the extent to which the proposal shows the potential impact of the project, making reference to:

- the relevance and appropriateness of any beneficiaries or collaborators
- whether appropriate routes and resources have been identified for dissemination and knowledge exchange

Please comment on the applicant's ability to deliver the proposed project, making reference to the:

- appropriateness of the track record of the applicant/s
- balance of skills of the project team, including academic collaborators

Please comment on the effectiveness of the proposed planning and management and on whether the requested resources are appropriate and have been fully justified.

When making their assessments, reviewers are asked to indicate level of confidence in their judgements. They are also asked to make an overall recommendation as to whether or not the project should be funded.

APPENDIX 5

Criteria used by NERC to assess responsive mode applications

- Excellence: with referees being asked to classify the proposed research on a seven point scale, ranging from reject, through Beta (probably not advancing the field) to Alpha-5 Outstanding (exceptional scientific merit and originality; expect to have major impact; top 5 per cent). This will include commenting on the importance of the research questions, the originality of the proposed research, and the soundness and feasibility of the proposed approach;
- Fit to NERC priorities: with referees being asked to classify the proposed research on a five point scale, ranging from E (not aligned with NERC priorities) to A (completely aligned with NERC's highest scientific priorities);
- Risk–Reward: graded on a two-dimensional matrix (with risk on one dimension and reward on the other, each with three levels). The reward dimension ranges from low (little probable long term impact on knowledge within environmental sciences) to high (certain long term, broad impact on knowledge within environmental sciences). The risk dimension ranges from low (no discernible operational risk) to high (likely operational risk. Risk that the proponents cannot carry out the research);
- Cost effectiveness: graded on a five point scale, ranging from I (poor value for money) to V (excellent value for money). You should note that 'value for money' is not the same as 'inexpensive' – a 'cheap' proposal can be poor value for money, just as a 'costly' proposal can be good value for money;
- Project-partner involvement (where relevant);
- Knowledge exchange plan, graded on a three point scale;
- Justification of resources;
- Use of NERC facilities (where relevant).

APPENDIX 6

Criteria used by BBSRC to assess responsive mode applications

- Scientific excellence: with referees being asked to comment on the extent to which the proposal meets the highest international standards of current research in its field, in terms of the proposed science and the suitability of the research team to undertake it and the research environment to support it;
- Strategic relevance: with referees commenting on relevance to BBSRC strategy, as well as to the needs of industry or other stakeholders;
- Economic and social impact: with referees being asked to comment on the extent to which the research will contribute knowledge that shows direct potential for economic return or societal benefits to the UK;
- Timeliness and promise: with referees commenting on the extent to which the application is particularly appropriate at the present time, or offers longer term benefits over and above the direct value of the research;
- Cost effectiveness: with referees being asked to comment on the extent to which the resources requested, relative to anticipated scientific gains, represent an attractive investment of BBSRC funds;
- Staff training potential of the project: where funding is requested to support research staff, referees are asked to comment on the extent to which the proposed project will provide research training and development opportunities of benefit to the individual to be employed and the wider science base.

Applicants are also asked to note any specific points (e.g. in relation to the use of animals, design of specific experiments) that need to be considered by the committee. Finally, they are asked to rate the proposal in terms of its overall competitiveness in international quality science, as being in the top 10 per cent, 20 per cent, 50 per cent, internationally competitive, nationally competitive, or not competitive.

APPENDIX 7

Criteria used by AHRC to assess responsive mode applications

Quality and Importance

- extent to which the proposal meets the specific aims of the scheme;
- significance and importance of the project, and the contribution it will make to enhancing or developing creativity, insight, knowledge or understanding of the area to be studied in a national or international context;
- extent to which the research questions, issues or problems are defined, and their appropriateness and importance specified;
- appropriateness of research context and specification of why it is important that these particular questions are addressed. Extent to which the current research in the area has been considered, and range of audiences targeted;
- appropriateness, effectiveness, and feasibility of proposed research methods/approach.

People

- quality and importance of work to date;
- ability to monitor the project and bring it to completion;
- appropriateness of the level and balance of any staffing on the project;
- whether any other named participants have appropriate experience and expertise.

Management of Project

- whether lines of responsibility and accountability are clearly articulated;
- whether the timescale is realistic and appropriate milestones incorporated;

- extent to which sufficient time and resources have been allowed for.

Value for Money

- extent to which the likely outcome of research will represent value for money;
- whether resources requested are reasonable in the context of the proposed research.

Collaboration/Dissemination

- appropriateness and effectiveness of proposed dissemination methods;
- likelihood that outputs and outcomes of the project will be highly valued and widely exploited, both in the research community and in wider contexts.

Applications are given an overall score on a scale from 1 (a proposal of an unsatisfactory level of originality, quality and significance, which does not meet the assessment criteria for the scheme, and does not provide satisfactory evidence and justification for the proposal; it is not suitable for funding) to 6 (an outstanding proposal meeting world class standards of scholarship, originality, quality, and significance; it fully meets all the assessment criteria for the scheme and provides full and consistent evidence and justification for the proposal; it should be funded as a matter of the very highest priority).

APPENDIX 8

Examples of appropriately worded abstracts/short summary statements

Example 1 [1]

Localized areas of basal friction (sticky spots) are known to be a significant control on ice stream behaviour and shutdown, and hence on overall ice stream stability. Although of critical importance, they are difficult to observe and characterize beneath contemporary ice streams. We will overcome this problem by using Earth Observation and fieldwork to map and characterize their distribution on three exposed former ice stream beds in Arctic Canada. This will provide the first physical description of the nature and occurrence of sticky ice spots including geologic, topographic and geotechnical data on their dimensions, geomorphology and distribution. Incorporated into a GIS, this data will be used to test existing numerical models of ice stream basal mechanics and shutdown in order to examine sticky spot influence on ice stream functioning.

Example 2 [2]

Delays in the planning process are widely recognized as contributing towards a shortfall in housing supply, which in turn has a negative effect on regional and national competitiveness. Despite some successes in speeding up the planning system in recent years, delays persist. One of the problems is the lack of good data and analysis of it with which to understand where and why such delays occur. This project will, for the first time, explain and identify the nature of the planning delay through creating and analysing a unique dataset on the planning process. Combining hedonic regression analysis with interviews of key actors in the development process to understand the contextual and behavioural characteristics of delay, the research will throw considerable light on the influence of the planning process over a range of housing development characteristics and types.

Example 3

It is becoming increasingly recognized that a healthy diet is crucial for healthy ageing. In recent years interest has grown in a class of compounds called provonals. Dietary intervention studies, using coffee, cocoa and, more recently, redcurrants, have begun to demonstrate beneficial effects of provonals on human cognitive performance, particularly in older adults. Building on human and animal work conducted in our laboratory, this multidisciplinary study will determine how specific provonals enhance decision-making performance in older adults, using both behaviour studies and fMRI imaging. The findings of this project have important implications for exploiting the potential beneficial effects of provonal components in the diet, particularly in relation to counteracting age-related decline in human decision-making performance.

Notes

1 I am grateful to Dr Christopher Stokes for allowing me to include this summary statement from one of his successful grant applications.
2 I am grateful to Professor Michael Ball for allowing me to include this summary statement from one of his successful grant applications.

APPENDIX 9

Further examples of cost justification statements

We have included technical assistance on this project as neither of the applicants is, or has the time to become, proficient in the kind of programming required (C+) for the software we need. This will enable us to tailor the design of the experiments in a way that would not be possible using commercially available presentation software. We estimate that the three experiments will require a total of 150 hours of programming time, at £7.50 per hour.

The major cost under consumables and exceptional items is for funding for the experimental participants to take part in the proposed studies. We estimate that the five experiments, together, will require a total of 300 participant sessions at £5 per session.

A dedicated PC is also needed for running the proposed experiments.

We request funds for fMRI scanning time and a contribution towards running and maintaining the scanner. This has been set at £380 per hour by the University of Berkshire's finance department. We anticipate that we will require one hour's scanning time for each of 20 people, totally £7600.

Resources are requested to support the annual review meetings that will be based either in the UK (one meeting) or Canada (two meetings). Funds are therefore requested for travel between Manchester and Montreal (for the PI and senior postdoc) to enable these important project planning discussions and knowledge exchanges to take place. The face-to-face meetings will be complemented by bi-monthly review meetings held via videoconferencing facilities. Additional funding is therefore requested to upgrade our video-conferencing facilities.

We request funding for 2 hours per week for each of the PI and Co-Investigator. This time will primarily be devoted to holding regular project meetings, additional project problem solving as required, dealing with project-related administrative matters, and for preparing conference presentations and journal articles that arise from the project, as well as the final project report.

APPENDIX 10

Further examples of appropriately worded dissemination statements

Example 1

The results of this research will be of interest to fellow researchers, teachers, educational psychologists and other practitioners, and parents. They will be disseminated through international refereed journals (such as *Child Development* and *Journal of Language and Memory*) and national and international conferences (such as the British Psychological Society Developmental Section annual meeting, and the International Conference on Research into Reading). The findings will also be presented to local teachers and parents at conventions run by the Dyslexia Association, and will be summarized in the Association's House Magazine. Further dissemination will take place through the University's public lecture programme.

Example 2

The results of this work will be disseminated through publication in international refereed journals, such as the *Journal of Experimental Psychology: Learning, Memory, and Cognition*, as well as through conference presentations, such as at meetings of the Experimental Psychology Society and European Conference on Cognitive Psychology. They will also be presented at meetings of the British Psychological Society which are attended by practitioners as well as academic psychologists. Scientists at Qinetiq have expressed interest in our work, and we are currently discussing our ideas with them.

Example 3

Findings from this project will be disseminated to fellow academics through conference presentations at appropriate national and international meetings, and by publication in leading journals such as the *Economic Journal* and *Journal of Banking and Finance*. We currently anticipate that around four academic journal articles and a jointly authored book will arise from this work. The datasets produced by the project will be made available to the UK data archive and on our Research Centre's website. We believe that the proposed project will also be of interest to the wider public, and we will liaise with our university's press office to issue a press release to the local and national media. We also plan to hold a workshop, hosted in our Research Centre, aimed at relevant practitioners working in the finance sector.

APPENDIX 11

Example of a summary statement at the end of a case for support

In summary, this project aims to resolve a number of questions concerning the properties and underlying mechanisms of the mere exposure effect. The first aim is to clarify the extent to which the mere exposure effect should be considered to be an implicit memory phenomenon. The second is to elucidate the processes present in the mere exposure effect, and how they differ from those in the non-affective versions of the task. This should facilitate the positioning of the mere exposure effect, relative to implicit memory tasks, along a perceptual/conceptual processing continuum. Overall, the main strength of the project is that it will bring together these two relatively independent fields of research, which should have both theoretical and practical benefits. First, integrating the mere exposure effect within an established implicit memory framework should help to provide a stronger theoretical explanation for a previously elusive phenomenon. Second, establishing that the mere exposure effect is an implicit memory phenomenon will provide not only an additional implicit memory measure but also a more ecologically valid one. This is important because it should help to stimulate research concerning how implicit memory affects behaviour in the real world. In the longer term, this may even promote the development of links between implicit memory and areas in social cognition, such as stereotype formation. Finally, the current project is particularly suited to a relatively inexpensive one-year study, as much of the necessary pilot work has been carried out. A suite of easily modifiable computer programs for running the experiments exists, and we would be in a position to start collecting data within a few weeks of the start of the project. The investigators are experienced researchers in the area of implicit memory, and are supported by the Learning and Memory research group at the Berkshire Psychology Department (5 rated in RAE 2001).

APPENDIX 12

Extracts from comments made by reviewers, with suggested responses

The investigators should remove all markers of oxidative stress from the study design and reduce the budget to reflect this.

Although we believe that it would be valuable to make these assessments in relation to the intervention, they are not a critical aspect of our study. We will therefore remove them from the design and recost the budget accordingly.

The investigators should use a lighter touch dietary assessment method such as 24 hour recall and 48 hour recalls rather than the proposed weekly diaries.

We are happy to replace the weekly food intake diaries with telephone calls to participants after 24 and 48 hours. We will use a multiple pass recall measure that we have used in previous studies (e.g. Jones and Smith, 2006). This will allow us to assess any reductions in red meat consumption and any increases in fruit and vegetable consumption by participants since the intervention.

Some components of this work would be better suited to an EPSRC directed proposal.

Last year we received specific advice from EPSRC that this project is more in NERC's remit than their own, and we also believe that the project addresses a pressing scientific issue that is central to NERC's remit. Our previous sound pollution project, which fed into the development of the proposed work, was also funded by NERC.

How certain are the investigators of there being sufficient involvement from the scientists based at the Haiti site?

We have worked with the scientists at the Haiti site for five years now. During the period we have conducted three field campaigns in which they have played a critical role. The three leading scientists at the site are co-authors on the four publications that have stemmed from the work to date. Two of their team have also visited our department during the past three years. We therefore know the team well and are absolutely confident of their full engagement and level of contribution.

Jones and Jones (2002) showed that pre-treatment indices of parental frustration are more predictive of outcomes than parental psychopathology, so it is not clear why the investigators are using the latter.

Unfortunately, this comment is rather misleading. The Jones and Jones study was not a child study (as ours is) but a family based study covering a wide range of age ranges. Interestingly, although parental anxiety was only cursorily assessed in the Jones and Jones study, the findings are not actually at odds with our hypothesis that parental anxiety is an impediment to child outcome IF it is not clinically treated.

As the processes of change in parent-child interactions may have a more long-term effect on the social and cognitive development of young children, it might be better to utilize a longer term follow up of at least two years.

In our proposal we suggested using a follow-up assessment after nine months, as this seems to be the minimum time that is feasible to assess the durability of any treatment effects. Clearly, it would be interesting to know more about any longer term effects. However, to add a two-year follow-on assessment to our design, as the referee suggests, would considerably extend the duration of the project and involve substantial additional cost. This does not seem justified to us.

How are the investigators sure they will be able to recruit sufficient eligible patients?

Our plan is to recruit 150 patients over 36 months. As detailed in our application, we have been running an adult sleep research clinic in our institute for the past four years and therefore have a firm basis for our estimation of the number of referrals that are likely to be made. Our considerable experience of running research in this and similar clinics underpins our statement that we anticipate that very few patients will decline the invitation to participate in the study, nor drop out during the course of the project. We therefore have confidence in both the proposed size of our sample and our estimated drop out rate.

APPENDIX 13

Example of content of information sheet given to patients in a questionnaire study

A questionnaire about whether or not the wording of an information sheet about the arthritis drug Methotrexate would influence your decision to take the drug or not

You are being invited to take part in a research study. Before you decide, it is important for you to understand why the research is being done and what it will involve. Please take time to read the following information carefully. Please ask if there is anything that is not clear or if you would like more information. Please take time to decide whether or not you wish to take part. Thank you for reading this.

The purpose of the study: Information leaflets containing information about the risks of particular treatments are now usually given to patients before starting treatment. However these information leaflets often contain little if any information about the benefits of the treatment, or indeed about the risks of *not* taking the treatment.

Many patients with rheumatoid arthritis attending this clinic are prescribed a drug called Methotrexate. We are conducting this research to see whether the wording of the leaflet governs how comfortable people would feel about taking Methotrexate, IF they had been diagnosed with rheumatoid arthritis and were prescribed this medicine.

You have been chosen for the study because you have been referred to this clinic for diagnosis and possible treatment of a painful condition of the bones, joints or muscles. This research does NOT assume that your painful condition is due to rheumatoid arthritis. However, we believe that as somebody suffering from pain you are better able than other members of the public to put yourself into the position of a patient with rheumatoid arthritis.

Why is this study being undertaken with people who do not have rheumatoid arthritis? Ideally we would like to undertake this research with people who have rheumatoid arthritis who are considering Methotrexate treatment. However, we need to get the views of many people, and there are simply not enough people who have rheumatoid arthritis who are considering Methotrexate treatment to complete the research within a reasonable time.

What if you are already taking Methotrexate? In that case you should not take part in this study.

What will happen to you if you take part? If you decide to take part, you will be given this information sheet to keep. You will also be asked to sign a consent form. The information collected in the study will be kept separate from your case notes and will not be looked at until the end of the study when sufficient questionnaires have been collected. Your GP will not be informed about your participation in the research.

When you arrive at the clinic you will be asked to complete a questionnaire which will take around five to ten minutes. You should return the completed questionnaire to the reception desk. You will then be seen as usual in the clinic. There will be no extra delay, no extra clinic visits and no extra blood tests or X-rays as a result of this research. If you change your mind while completing the questionnaire, and decide not to take part after all, simply return the partly completed questionnaire to the reception desk.

What will happen if you decide not to take part? It is up to you whether you take part in the study or not. If you decide not to take part, please return the questionnaire uncompleted to the reception desk. You will be seen as usual in the clinic and your consultation and treatment will be in no way different from those who agree to complete the questionnaire. The clinic doctor will not know whether or not you have completed the questionnaire.

Confidentiality: We are interested in the results of a whole group of people, not individual results. Questionnaires and those who completed them will not be identified by any system except by your signature on the consent form; the questionnaire results will be separated from the consent form, then taken and analysed together, so that we will not know who completed which questionnaires. We will however keep all completed copies of the questionnaire.

Afterwards: You may request a copy of any published study that appears as a result of this research.

APPENDIX 14

Example of a standard outline consent form for use in research studies

Outline consent form

1 I have read and had explained to me by .... the accompanying Information Sheet relating to the project on ....
2 I have had explained to me the purposes of the project and what will be required of me, and any questions I have had have been answered to my satisfaction. I agree to the arrangements described in the Information Sheet in so far as they relate to my participation.
3 I understand that participation is entirely voluntary and that I have the right to withdraw from the project at any time, and that this will be without detriment to any care or services I may be receiving or may receive in the future.
4 (If appropriate) I authorize the investigator to consult my General Practitioner and I authorize my General Practitioner to disclose any information which may be relevant to my proposed participation in the project.
5 This application has been reviewed by the ....Research Ethics Committee and has been given a favourable ethical opinion for conduct.
6 I have received a copy of this Consent Form and of the accompanying Information Sheet.

Name

Date of Birth (if relevant)

Signed

Date

APPENDIX 15

Examples of completed financial sections of a Je-S application form

Summary of resources required

Summary fund heading	Fund heading	Full economic cost	BBSRC contribution	% BBSRC contribution
Directly incurred	Staff	36 017	28 813	80
	Travel and subsistence	4600	3680	80
	Equipment			
	Other costs	16 885	13 508	80
	Sub total	57 502	46 001	
Directly allocated	Investigators	9860	7888	80
	Staff	6632	5305	80
	Estates costs	42 560	34 048	80
	Other directly allocated costs			
	Sub total	59 052	47 241	
Indirect costs	Indirect costs	128 850	103 080	
Exceptions	Staff			
	Other costs			
	Sub total			
	Total	245 404	196 322	

Role	Basic starting salary	Scale	Increment date	Start date	Period on project	% full time	Sup. + NI	Other allowances	Total cost on grant
Researcher	RA (tba) 29 704	Gr. 6 pt 30	1.10.2011	1.10.10	36mths	100	6313		36 017

Directly allocated posts: applicants

Role	Name	Post will outlast project	Contracted working week as % of ft work	Total no. of hours to be charged to grant	Average number of hours per week charged to grant	Rate of salary pool/banding	Cost estimate
PI	Dr Smith	Yes	100%	528	4	Gr. 8	6900
Co-I	Dr Bloggs	Yes	100%	264	2	Gr. 7	2960

Technician

Role	Basic starting salary	Scale	Increment date	Start date	Period on project	% full time	Sup. + NI	Other allowances	Total cost on grant
Technician	(tba) 25 623	Gr. 5 pt 25	1.1.2012	1.1.2011	24mths	20	7537		6632

Travel and subsistence

Destination and purpose		Total cost
Within UK	Annual neurodegeneration conference, Cambridge. September 2011. Costs for PI and RA to attend	£1600
Outside UK	Annual neuroscience conference, Oregon, US. September 2012. Costs for PI and RA to attend	£3000
		£4600

Other directly incurred costs

Description	Total £
RMI PC for Research Assistant	1855
17" CRT monitor	180
HP Colour printer	280
Use of BioAnalyser. 40 runs @ £38 per run	1520
Software licences	850
Cell culture Plastic ware	4000
Cell culture reagents	5200
Other laboratory consumables	3000
Total	16 885

References

Abreu, M., Grinevich, V., Hughes, A., Kitson, M. and Termouth, P. (2008) *Universities, Business and Knowledge Exchange*. London: Council for Industry and Higher Education and Centre for Business Research.

Abreu, M., Grinevich, V., Kitson, M. and Savona, M. (2008) *Absorptive Capacity and Regional Patterns of Innovation*. London: DIUS.

Adams, J. and Bekhradnia, B. (2004) *What Future for Dual Support?* Higher Education Policy Institute report.

Association of Commonwealth Universities (2008) Association of Commonwealth Universities and Global Research Management Network, Research Management Survey. London: ACU/GRMN.

Ball, S. (2007) Leadership of academics in research, *Educational Management, Administration and Leadership*, 35: 449–77.

Bazeley, P. (2003) Defining 'early career' in research, *Higher Education*, 45: 257–79.

Beecher, H.K. (1966) Consent in clinical experimentation; myth and reality, *Journal of the American Medical Association*, 195: 34–5.

Boucher, C., Smyth, A. and Johnstone, M. (2004) Creating Collaborative Spaces: The Pleasures and Perils of Doing Multi-disciplinary, Multi-partner Qualitative Research. *Journal of Higher Education Policy and Management*, 26: 419–28.

Brown, R. (2007) *International Competitiveness and the Role of Universities*. London: The Council for Industry and Higher Education.

Burman, R. and Evans, A.J. (2008) Target Zero. A culture of safety, *Defence Aviation Safety Centre Journal*, 1: 22–7.

Bushaway, R.W. (2003) *Managing Research*. Maidenhead: Open University Press.

Calvert, J. (2004) The idea of 'basic research' in language and practice, *Minerva*, 42: 251–68.

Cicchetti, D.V. (1991) The reliability of peer review for manuscript and grant submissions: a cross-disciplinary investigation, *Behavioral and Brain Sciences*, 14: 119–35.

Clark, B.R. (1994) The research–teaching nexus in modern systems of higher education, *Higher Education Policy*, 7: 11–17.

Cyert, R.M. and Goodman, P.S. (1997) Creating effective university–industry alliances; an organizational learning perspective, *Organizational Dynamics*, 25: 45–57.

D'Este, P.D. and Patel, D. (2007) University–industry linkages in the UK; what are the factors underlying the variety of interactions with industry? *Research Policy*, 36: 1295–313.

EPSRC (2009) Including economic impact in funding applications. www.epsrc.ac.uk/researchfunding/changes/economicimpact.htm (accessed July 2009).

ESRC (2009) Economic and Social Research Council. www.esrc.ac.uk (accessed July 2009).

Evidence (2005) Impact of selective funding of research in England, and the specific outcomes of HEFCE research funding. Evidence Report, September.

Gitlin, L.N. and Lyons, K.J. (2008) *Successful Grant Writing: Strategies for Health and Human Service Professionals*, 3rd edn. New York: Springer.

Green, J. and Langley, D. (2009) Professionalising Research Management. Report for HEFCE and MRC, Spring 2009. www.professionalisingresearchmanagement.com (accessed June 2009).

Harvie, D. (2000) Alienation, class and enclosure in UK universities, *Capital and Class*, 71: 103–32.

HEFCE (2005) Joint Costing and Pricing Steering Group. Transparent Approach to Costing: An Overview of TRAC. JM Consulting. Bristol: HEFCE.

HEFCE (2006) Future needs for capital funding in Higher Education; A review of the future of SRIF and learning and teaching capital. A report by JM Consulting. Higher Education Funding Council for England. Research and Evaluation Report September 2006. Bristol: HEFCE.

HEFCE (2008) Counting what is measured or measuring what counts; league tables and their impact on Higher Education Institutions in England. Higher Education Funding Council for England. Report 2008/14. Bristol: HEFCE.

HEFCE (2009) Higher Education – Business and Community Interaction Survey 2007–8. HEFCE Report 2009/23. Bristol: HEFCE.

Heller, R. (ed.) (2002) *Manager's Handbook*. London: Dorling Kindersley.

HM Treasury (2004) *Science and Innovation Investment Framework 2004–2014*. Norwich: HMSO.

HM Treasury (2006) *Science and Innovation Investment Framework 2004–2014. Next Steps*. Norwich: HMSO.

Human Tissue Authority (2004) *Human Tissue Act*. www.hta.gov.uk

Jayasinghe, U.W., Marsh, H.W. and Bond, N. (2003) A multi-level cross-classifying approach to peer review of grant proposals. The effects of assessor and researcher attributes on assessor ratings, *Journal of the Royal Statistical Society* (A), 166: 279–300.

Johnson, A.M. (2009) *Charting a Course for a Successful Research Career: A Guide for Early Career Researchers*. Amsterdam: Elsevier.

Kenway, J., Boden, R. and Epstein, D. (2007) *Winning and Managing Research Funding: The Academic's Support Kit*. London: Sage.

Lambert, R. (2003) Lambert Review of Business–University Collaboration. Final Report. HM Treasury. London, UK.

Laudel, G. (2006) The quality myth; promoting and hindering conditions for acquiring research funds, *Higher Education*, 52: 375–403.

Lowe, P. and Philipson, J. (2006) Reflexive interdisciplinary research; the making of a research programme on the Rural Economy and Land Use, *Journal of Agricultura Research*, 57: 165–84.

Lucas, L. (2006) *The Research Game in Academic Life*. Maidenhead: Open University Press, SRHE.

Marsh, H.W. and Ball, S. (1991) Reflections on the peer review process, *Behavioral and Brain Sciences*, 14: 157–8.

Marsh, H.W., Bond, N. and Jayasinghe, U.W. (2007) Peer review process; assessments by applicant nominated referees are biased, inflated, unreliable and invalid, *Australian Psychologist*, 42: 33–8.

Marsh, H.W., Jayasinghe, U.W. and Bond, N. (2008) Improving the peer review proces for grant applications, *American Psychologist*, April: 160–8.

OECD (2002) *Frascati Manual. Proposed Standard Practice for Surveys of Research and Experimental Development*. Paris: OECD.

Ortmann, A. and Hertwig, R. (1997) Is deception acceptable? *American Psychologist*, 52: 746–7.

OST (2004) *University Research Sustainability*. www.ost.gov.uk/research/dualsupport.htm (accessed January 2009).

Prigge, G.W. (2005) University–industry partnerships: what do they mean to universities? *Industry and Higher Education*, 19: 221.

RCUK (2007a) *Research Councils UK Delivery Plan 2008/09 to 2010/11*. www.rcuk.ac.uk/cmsweb/downloads/rcuk/publications/2009deliveryplan.pdf (accessed December 2007).

RCUK (2007b) *Research Councils UK Efficiency and Value for Money of Peer Review Project. Response to project report and consultation*. www.rcuk.ac.uk/research/peer/efficiencypr.htm (accessed February 2009).

RCUK (2009) *Policy and Code of Conduct on the Governance of Good Research Conduct: Integrity, Clarity and Good Management*. (rcuk.ac.uk July 2009).

Ries, J.B. and Leukefeld, C.G. (1998) *The Research Funding Guidebook: Getting It, Managing It, and Renewing It*. Thousand Oaks, CA: Sage.

Sandler, J.C. and Russell, B.L. (2005) Faculty student collaborations: ethics and satisfaction in authorship credit, *Ethics and Behaviour*, 15: 65–80.

Skingle, M. (2000) Forging industrial–academic links. ResearchResearch Funding Guide. www.researchresearch.com (accessed 21 January 2000).

Smith, R. (1992) Audit and research, *British Medical Journal*, 305: 905.

THE (2008) *Times Higher Education Supplement*. 1,868, 16.

UKRIO (2009) *Code of Practice for Research: Promoting Good Practice and Preventing Misconduct*. www.ukrio.org (September 2009).

Valentin, E.M. (2000) University-industry co-operation: a framework of benefits and obstacles, *Industry and Higher Education*, 14: 165–72.

Ward, D. (2009) Address to Annual HEFCE Conference, Royal Holloway University, April.

Wenneras, C. and World, A. (1999) Bias in peer review of research proposals, in F. Godless and T. Jefferson (eds) *Peer Review in Health Science*. London: BMJ Books.

World Medical Association (1975) *The Declaration of Helsinki*. Tokyo, Japan, October.

World Medical Association (2008) *The Declaration of Helsinki*, 6th edn. Seoul, 2008.

Zinser, E.A. (1985) Potential conflict of interest issues in relationships between academia and industry, in J.B. Bennett and J.W. Peltason (eds) *Contemporary Issues in Higher Education*. New York: Macmillan.

Author Index

Subject Index